Creative Synchronized Swimming

Creative Synchronized Swimming

Beulah O. Gundling
Jill E. White

International Academy of Aquatic Art

LEISURE PRESS
Champaign, Illinois

Library of Congress Cataloging-in-Publication Data

Gundling, Beulah O., 1916-
  Creative synchronized swimming.

  Bibliography: p.
  Includes index.
  1. Synchronized swimming. 2. Synchronized swimming—
Coaching. I. White, Jill E., 1955-   . II. Title.
GV838.53.S95G86   1988   797.2′1′07   87-17049
ISBN 0-88011-299-9

Developmental Editor: Sue Ingels Mauck
Copy Editor: Patrick O'Hayer
Assistant Editors: JoAnne Cline and Phaedra Hise
Production Director: Ernie Noa
Projects Manager: Lezli Harris
Typesetter: Sandra Meier
Text Design: Keith Blomberg
Text Layout: Denise Mueller
Cover Design: Conundrum Designs
Illustrations By: Cathie Barefoot and Gaby Moffitt
Printed By: Versa Press

ISBN: 0-88011-299-9

Printed in the United States of America

10 9 8 7 6 5 4 3 2 1

Leisure Press
A Division of Human Kinetics Publishers, Inc.
Box 5076, Champaign, IL 61820
1-800-DIAL-HKP
1-800-334-3665 (in Illinois)

To my husband, Henry I. Gundling, who has helped me and many others to reap the rewards of a creative aquatic activity.

Beulah O. Gundling

To all the swimmers who have known the exuberant joys of creating and performing; and to the coaches and teachers who inspire creative movement and motivate swimmers to excellence.

Jill E. White

Contents

Preface

Unique movements and expression can improve any performance. This book is designed to stimulate your creativity, encourage the use of aquatic skills for artistic expression, and instruct you in ways to improve technique. Anyone interested in being creative with aquatic movement—from coaches and performers to recreational swimmers—will enjoy the ideas we will present.

The explanations of the variations are kept as brief as possible. We assume that the reader is already familiar with the basic skills and common techniques of synchronized swimming and can execute the majority of Standard Figures with at least average proficiency. Standard Figures are those listed in the *Official Synchronized Swimming Handbook* (VanBuskirk & Scandaliato, 1985) for use in competition. Each Figure has a difficulty rating and a standard method of execution.

Many of the Standard Figures used today were originally figure variations that became popular enough to be included among the listed figures. Although Standard Figures must be executed exactly as stated in the rules during competition, other styles of execution are possible and desirable in other situations.

Swimmers and coaches often use the term *hybrid* to describe the types of variations we will be describing, especially when they refer to figures. Because this book contains many types of aquatic movement in addition to figures, we will use the term *variation* instead of hybrid.

Variation possibilities are practically unlimited, and a book could be devoted exclusively to one type, such as Ballet Leg variations. However, we will describe selective examples of figures and movements that will help you enlarge your aquatic vocabulary, increase your proficiency in the water, and stimulate you to discover additional variations.

Describing movement so that it is accurately understood by everyone is very difficult. In addition, every technique must be at least somewhat adapted to fit each individual's different body structure. A movement of the arms used in the execution of a figure, for example, may not be the same for everyone; it may vary according to position, depth, range, force, and even type of movement. The descriptions and illustrations will be a guide for the sequence of movement involved, but it is up to you to experiment to discover the adaptations that are necessary for you. You will find that creating aquatic variations is challenging, stimulating, and fun.

Each of the five parts of this book focuses on a particular form of aquatic variation. Part I ("Fun With Movement") supplies you with introductory material and techniques for getting your creative ideas flowing. Part II ("Fun With Variations for One Swimmer") contains figure and stroke variations that do not need a partner or group to perform, although they could certainly be synchronized with other swimmers. Part III ("Fun With Variations for More Than One Swimmer") is for duets, groups, and teams; it includes contact figures, stroking and floating patterns, lifts, and variations that need more than one swimmer to perform. Parts IV ("Fun With Warm-Ups and Technique Drills") and V ("Fun With Performing and Creating") are for every swimmer interested in improving technique through training variations and performing those skills before an audience.

Find the section that contains the type of skills you would like to develop, and enjoy!

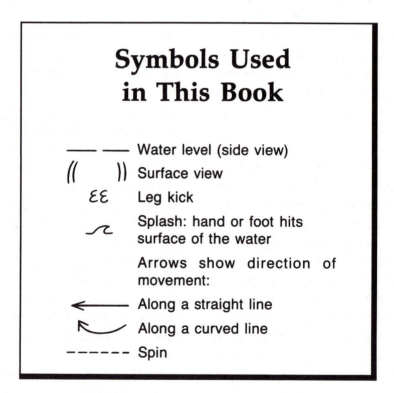

Symbols Used in This Book

—— —— Water level (side view)

(( )) Surface view

ƐƐ Leg kick

Splash: hand or foot hits surface of the water

Arrows show direction of movement:

←—— Along a straight line

↰ Along a curved line

------ Spin

Part I
Fun With Movement

Chapter 1

Introductory Information

Those of you who have read Lewis Carroll's *Through the Looking Glass* will remember that Alice found things reversed on the other side of the looking glass. This situation is quite similar to the one you will find when you step from your natural environment into a new world—a world of water.

In learning to swim you have already encountered some of the reversals. Your locomotion on land occurs primarily with the body in an upright (vertical) position. In the water it is much easier to move lying down, with the body horizontal. On land your legs furnish the means of locomotion, but your arms may provide the main or sole source of propulsive power in water. If you pull your arms through the water in the direction of your feet, you move headfirst. To move feetfirst, you must scoop the water in the direction of the head. You must press down to rise and press up to descend. To somersault forward, the arms circle backward, and to somersault backward, they circle forward. If you study ballet, you know that a quick inward movement of the right arm across

the front of the body helps you to pirouette to the left. But if you do the same movement in the water, you will turn to the right. In water you can defy Newton's law of gravity because a greater effort is required to sink the body than to raise it. However, if you lift any part of the body above the surface, then what goes up must come down.

In addition to things being reversed, Alice found the world beyond the looking glass strange—full of surprises and the unexpected. You will find a similar situation in the world of water, and some of these surprises may be considered disadvantages. For example, you cannot move as quickly through water as you can on land. You cannot breathe underwater, and the length of time you can stay below the surface is therefore limited. Even on the water surface your natural and instinctive breathing habits must be changed. Mouth breathing, frowned upon on land, becomes a necessity in water. The eyes are irritated by water and are unable to see as clearly underwater as on land. Moreover, to move the body in water requires more effort and a greater expenditure of energy than on land.

Yet these disadvantages are only minor in comparison with the advantages. Because the water offers more resistance to movement than air, it is necessary to breathe deeply, increasing lung capacity and providing more oxygen for the body. The water pressure, when accompanied by movement, is soothing and gently massages the body.

Although some movements may be more difficult in water than on land, others, such as standing on the hands, are easier. And many activities are possible in water that are impossible on land. Have you ever tried to float on air? It is impossible, of course, because the body is too heavy. But you do not have to zoom off into outer space to experience weightlessness—just head for the nearest swimming pool. The body achieves a quality of weightlessness in the water, enabling you to float in a number of different positions, even upside down.

You cannot go below the surface on land without first digging a hole, but you can easily go below the water surface to different depths. In the water your walking, running, or leaping is limited to slow motion; nevertheless, you have a great variety of other means of propulsion from which to choose. You can stroke, scull, twist, spiral, turntable, roll, somersault, flip, and even lift both legs into the air without worrying about falling or injuring yourself. You can move in any direction and with a much greater variety of body positions than is possible on land.

Dives and stunts performed in the air must be executed extremely quickly; however, the properties of water permit you to perform these movements in slow motion, allowing you and the spectators more time to savor fully the pleasing sensation of controlled body action, to appreciate the difficulty involved, and to enjoy the beauty of the movement.

Thus we discover that the world of water is fascinating, exciting, and challenging for the aquatic artist. There is always something new to be discovered, something more to be learned and mastered. The world of water offers the aquatic artist new horizons, adventures, and rich treasures—no, not sunken gold and silver, but something even more precious: the joy of freedom of movement, the thrill that comes with acquiring control and mastery of the body in a new medium, and the stimulation that results from discovering expressive and beautiful aquatic movement.

In addition to the rewards offered by a creative and aesthetic activity, there are extra bonuses: the healthful benefits of a physical activity and the fun of a recreational one. Whatever your preferences may be, treasures are certainly waiting for you in the fascinating world of water.

In a lecture on "Integrity and Artistry in Composition," Peg Foster spoke of the potential that we have available to us when we work to develop skills in the water (cited in Gundling, 1964).

> Use the water! I can't emphasize this enough. Some people try to make the pool as much like a stage as possible when we have this marvelous advantage over a stage: We have a three-dimensional cube of clear fluid *in which* to work, *not on which* to work. This cube enables the human body to suspend itself in it, or to rise to the top of it, or to propel itself through it or across it. Use the sounds of the

water or the silences of the water, the fluidity of the water and the hardness of the water.

Use the buoyant force of the water. Think of all the movements you might do while the water slowly lifts you from the bottom. Use the sides and bottom of the pool for propulsion. It is beautiful to see bodies gliding gracefully through the water, the propulsion for which came from the bottom or sides of the pool. Rather than using the area beneath the surface for a disappearance act to conclude a movement, use it for its own sake.

In other words, use the properties of water to their fullest to best express your idea simply, directly, and without superfluous fill-in material. Express your idea to the best of your ability and then get out of the water. It is only coincidental if existing figures fulfill the demands of your ideas. Thus it is necessary to take a new look at aquatic movements and your "work space" in terms of their potentials and in terms of the simple things you already know.

You are very lucky to have the opportunity to create something that is artistic, aesthetically pleasing, and, most of all, your very own. Work within your limitations and have a wonderful time. Perhaps you may create an object of art, long to be remembered. (p. 177)

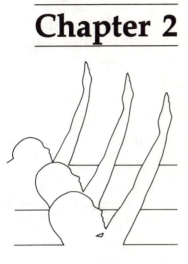

Chapter 2

The Alphabet of Aquatic Movement: Basic Positions, Movements, and Terms

Variations in the water are fun to originate and execute. They increase your enjoyment in the water, and they stimulate and challenge your imagination and skill.

Variations are especially useful in originating aquatic compositions, better enabling you to interpret music and carry out a theme than would be possible with only standard figures. Variations make a composition appear new, unique, and outstanding—if you have chosen original, appropriate variations and have performed them well.

The number of possibilities for variations is limited only by your own imagination and skill. Think of the thousands of words that can be made using only the letters of the alphabet. The alphabet of aquatic movement can be used in much the same way, but first, of course, it is necessary to learn this alphabet.

Body Positions

The positions may be performed below, above, or at the surface of the water. The body may be horizontal, vertical, inverted, or diagonal.

1. Layout: Body is straight from head through toes. The layout can be performed horizontally at the surface in a Back Layout, Front Layout, or Side Layout, and

it is frequently used as a starting and finishing position for figures. The layout can also be performed with the body in a Vertical, Inverted Vertical, or Diagonal position.

2. Arched: The back is arched, legs straight.
3. Tuck: The back is rounded, legs bent at hips and knees.
4. Pike: The body is bent at the hips, legs straight.

Basic Leg Positions

The legs can be moved to any position from any body position.

1. Legs together.
2. Legs crossed.
3. Bent Knee: One leg is straight, other leg is bent.
4. Split: V Split, Scissors Split, L Split.

Basic Arm Positions

The arms can be moved to any position from any body position.

1. At sides.
2. T position: Arms are extended sideways at shoulder level.
3. Overhead: Arms are in V position or are together with the edges of index fingers touching.

Basic Head Positions

1. Head in line with body.
2. Head forward.
3. Head backward.
4. Head turned to side.

Basic Body Movements

Without use of leg or arm movements below the surface of the water.

1. Floating or suspension movements.
2. Pendulum movements.
3. Rolling.
4. Stretching/contracting movements: tucking, piking, arching, twisting, and undulating the body, sometimes resulting in propulsion.

Basic Leg Movements

For propulsion, support, and balance.

1. Flutter Kick: performed on front, side, or back with body in any basic position; results in continuous propulsion or support.
2. Scissors Kick: performed with body horizontal, vertical, or diagonal; results in intermittent propulsion or support.
3. Breaststroke Kick: performed with body horizontal or diagonal; results in intermittent propulsion or support.
4. Dolphin Kick: performed on front, side, or back with body horizontal or diagonal; results in undulating propulsion.
5. Eggbeater Kick: performed with body vertical; results in continuous propulsion or support.
6. Marching: performed in vertical, horizontal, or side position and is a modified walking or bicycle type of movement that results in continuous propulsion.

Basic Sculling Arm Movements

For propulsion, support, and balance.

1. Flat Scull: Wrists are flat.
2. Standard Scull: Hands are bent backward from wrists.
3. Reverse Scull: Hands are bent forward from wrists.
4. Hybrid Scull: Less wrist bend occurs than with Standard or Reverse Sculls.
5. Support Scull: Modified Flat Scull performed with body in inverted position, palms facing bottom of pool.
6. Propeller (or Torpedo) Scull: Arms are overhead, and hands are in Standard or Hybrid position to move feetfirst; reverse to move headfirst.

Figure 2.1. Sculling Hand Positions

Basic Pulling Arm Movements

Keep palms and wrists flat.

1. Front Pull: Press arms toward feet and underneath body for headfirst propulsion.

2. Side Pull: Press arms sideways toward feet for headfirst propulsion.
3. Inward Pull: Press to or toward front of trunk from T position, ending with arms bent.
4. Outward Pull: Press from center of body outward to T position.

Basic Scoops

Keep palms and wrists flat.

1. Front Scoop: Press arms forward toward head for feetfirst propulsion.
2. Side Scoop: Press arms sideways toward head for feetfirst propulsion.

Finning

Finning is pushing the palms against the water to propel the body in the opposite direction of the push. Propulsion is intermittent if one or both arms are used simultaneously, and it is continuous if the arms are moved alternately.

Factors That Can Affect Positions or Movements

Many factors can influence the ability to effectively execute any of these positions or movements. Inhaling, exhaling, and holding the breath can affect propulsion and support. Moving the head forward, backward, or sideways can change the position of the body. Keep these ideas in mind if you seem to be having difficulty assuming and maintaining any position.

Remember, too, that arm movements can affect the body in different ways, depending on how they are executed. For example, if both arms move alternately when executing pulls and scoops, propulsion is continuous. If both arms move simultaneously, propulsion is intermittent. If only one arm is used, the body turns. These different types of propulsion can affect the appearance of the movement being performed and can be used very effectively when creating variations from the basic positions and movements.

Basic Terms You Should Know

1. Boat position: Back Layout with arms at sides, usually sculling.
2. Sailboat position: Boat with one leg in Bent Knee position, with thigh of bent leg vertical.

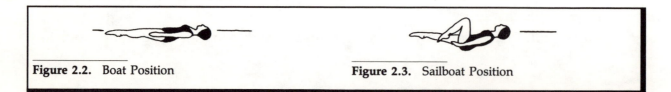

Figure 2.2. Boat Position   **Figure 2.3.** Sailboat Position

3. Spearfish (or Flamingo) position: A Ballet Leg varation.
4. Inverted Spearfish.
5. Inverted Pike (or Front Pike, Surface).
6. Inverted Tuck.
7. Fishtail: Body in Inverted Vertical, legs in L Split position, foot of horizontal leg at surface.

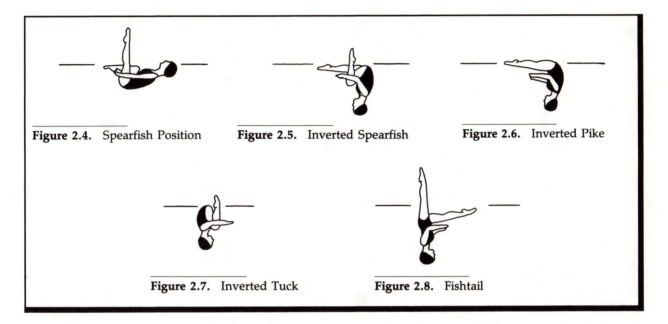

Figure 2.4. Spearfish Position   **Figure 2.5.** Inverted Spearfish   **Figure 2.6.** Inverted Pike

Figure 2.7. Inverted Tuck   **Figure 2.8.** Fishtail

8. Twist: The body turns in place at a constant level in either Inverted Vertical or Vertical position. A modified form of Support Scull may be used. To twist at a lower level in Inverted Vertical positions, the arms may be overhead, alternately making small circles. One hand makes an inward circle while the other hand makes an outward circle. Other techniques are possible.
9. Spin: The body turns in place while descending or rising in an Inverted Vertical or Vertical position. Spins are usually added when maximum height is reached. Techniques vary, but an Inverted Vertical Spin is usually performed following an outward movement of the arms in Support Scull. One arm does an Inward Pull; the other moves overhead to aid in balance, where it may be joined by the first arm after the Inward Pull.
10. Turntable: The horizontal body turns in place at or below the surface either at a constant level or while rising. An efficient way of doing a Turntable at the surface or while rising is to scull with the arms at the sides. One arm performs a Standard Scull, and the other arm a Reverse Scull. To Turntable at a constant level with the trunk below the surface, do Standard Scull with both arms. Keep one at the side, the other overhead, and the palms toward the surface to keep the body from rising.

Chapter 3

How to Originate Aquatic Variations

Originating variations is not difficult. Instead, it is interesting, stimulating, and most enjoyable. Variations usually come about by experimenting and by arranging the various letters of the aquatic alphabet in new combinations. Following are brief descriptions of some ways you can originate variations. These will be discussed in greater detail in future chapters.

1. Combine parts of two or more strokes or figures (chapters 4 and 14).
2. Change the start, middle section, or ending of a Standard Figure (chapter 5).
3. Use an unusual method of changing from one position to another (chapter 7).
4. Change the position of a part of the body, such as the head, arm, or leg, from that ordinarily used in a Standard Figure. Even a minor change, such as a difference in hand position or changing the angle or direction of a knee bend, alters the appearance and effect of a figure or skill (chapter 6).

5. Change the timing and/or force. A figure or skill performed slowly looks different from the same one performed quickly. Also, a figure or skill performed forcefully looks different from the same one performed with soft, flowing movements (chapter 10).

Further variations can be made by varying the speed and/or force within a figure or skill. For example, one part of the figure or skill can be performed slowly and smoothly, and another part quickly and forcefully. Such changes also affect the rhythm of the figure or skill, altering its appearance.

6. Reverse a figure. Some common examples are Forward Somersault-Backward Somersault, Forward Walkover-Backward Walkover, and Dolphin-Foot First Dolphin. Experiment not only with changing direction to reverse the figure but also reversing the order in which the figure is usually performed (chapter 5).

7. Repeat a figure or part of it, as in a Multiple Kip (chapter 5).

8. Add-on. Take a figure or skill and add to it one or more different figures or skills with no pauses between each (chapter 9).

9. Choose a position and see how many ways you can get into it and out of it (chapter 5).

10. Take an object and see what things you can do with it in the water (chapter 13).

11. Take movements from a land activity (dance, gymnastics, etc.) and adapt them into aquatic ones. This is very much like translating a sentence from one language into another, and it can seldom be done literally—certain changes have to be made to convey the original meaning. Translating movements from land activities into aquatic ones requires certain adaptations so that the original feeling and intent are conveyed. Knowledge of both forms of movement is required to do this successfully, as well as sensitivity and a willingness to experiment until the right effect is achieved (chapter 8).

12. Take a subject and try to interpret it with aquatic movements. The subject can be an object, a person, a place, an animal, a feeling, an activity, and so forth. The choice is limited only by your imagination. This is useful preparation for choreographing a composition in which you try to discover and use only movements that suggest or develop a theme you have selected (chapter 12).

13. Interpret accompaniment with movements that relate to a theme. The accompaniment and the theme together suggest certain types of movements, and the music suggests the rhythm, tempo, and quality of the movements. Such variations come about only after you have reached a thorough understanding of your theme and music and after you have spent considerable time thinking and experimenting. Discovering variations that are just right for you and your theme and accompaniment is very exciting (chapters 22 and 23).

Aquatic art compositions, in which you interpret your theme throughout, are much more satisfying to perform and are enjoyed more by the audience than routines that consist merely of a series of ordinary and meaningless figures, strokes, and other movements synchronized to music.

The ideas and exercises presented in this chapter are designed to get even the most "uncreative" swimmers to explore new ways of combining movements in the water. Once you get started, you will be surprised at the movements you can create and how easy and fun it is.

Part II
Fun With Variations for One Swimmer

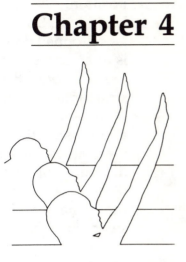

Chapter 4

Stroking and Sculling Variations for One Swimmer

Many variations are possible for all aquatic skills, and strokes are no exception. The more you experiment, the more variations you will discover. To help you get started, here are a few suggestions.

Changing Leg Movements or Their Rhythm

1. Use Flutter Kick with Elementary Backstroke, Inverted Breaststroke, Sidestroke, or Breaststroke.
2. Use orthodox Breaststroke Kick with the Butterfly Armstroke.
3. On back, hands on hips, use Flutter Kick but change rhythm: Do two slow Flutter Kicks (left, right; count 1, 2), four double-time Flutter Kicks (left, right, left, right; count 3, and, 4, and), and repeat. Do three slow Flutter Kicks (left, right, left; count 1, 2, 3) and six double-time Flutter Kicks (right, left, right, left, right, left; count 4, and, 5, and, 6, and).

Changing Arm Movements

1. Double-Arm Backstroke: Flutter Kick on back and instead of recovering arms alternately as in Back Crawl, raise both overhead together and pull to sides.
2. Side Overarm: Do Sidestroke and recover top arm out of the water.
3. Over-the-Waves Breaststroke: Do Breaststroke and recover the arms out of the water in front of the face,

making a half-circle pattern with fingertips before they enter the water, and extend in the glide position.

4. High-Arm: Do Front Crawl with the legs dropped down so that the body is at an angle in the water and the head is out. Bring the arm out straight and behind the body, then lift up and over the head so that the arm brushes the side of the head as it moves to enter the water directly in front of the shoulder. The Straight Arm stroke is performed the same way, except the arm is swept just above the surface of the water to the position in front of the shoulder.

5. Bent Arm: Do Front Crawl with legs dropped and head out but begin each stroke by ''popping'' the elbow out of the water first, lifting it higher than the head with the thumb next to the armpit. The hand then reaches straight forward to enter in front of the shoulder at any distance from the body. The opposite shoulder may need to drop slightly to enable you to get the elbow high enough so the hand clears the water when reaching forward.

6. Combining stroke types: Combine one Straight Arm with one Bent Arm, two High-Arms followed by two Straight Arms, and so on.

Changing the Hand Position

1. On Over-the-Waves Breaststroke, instead of recovering out of the water with thumb edges of hands touching, do one of the following: (a) Place palm of right hand over the back of the left hand, (b) place palms together, or (c) have palms facing up with edges of little fingers touching.

2. Use different hand positions to change the character and expressiveness of strokes. Experiment with a variety of different positions with any stroke in which the hand comes out of the water.

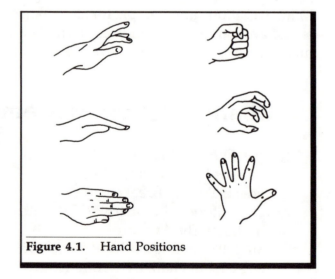

Figure 4.1.   Hand Positions

Combining Strokes

1. Breaststroke/Butterfly: Follow one Breaststroke with one Butterfly and repeat.

2. Breaststroke/Sidestroke: Do one Breaststroke. Start a second Breaststroke but end in the Glide position.

Do one Sidestroke. Start a second Sidestroke but finish in the Front Glide position.

3. Crawl/Back Crawl (Waltz Crawl): Do three Back Crawls, rolling onto face on third stroke, and do three

Front Crawls, rolling onto back on third stroke. You may also do this using four Crawls and four Back Crawls.

4. Revolving Crawl: Turn on each arm stroke so that the body revolves while doing the Crawl and Back Crawl.

Using a Roll

1. Corkscrew: Do a Sidestroke or Side Overarm and when in the glide position make a complete roll. Repeat.
2. Breaststroke Roll: Do Breaststroke and when in the glide position make a complete roll. Repeat.
3. Inverted Breaststroke Roll: Do Inverted Breaststroke and when in glide position make a complete roll. Repeat.
4. Inverted Breaststroke/Breaststroke Roll: Do Inverted Breaststroke and on glide make a half roll to Front Layout position. Do Breaststroke and on glide make a half roll to Back Layout position. Repeat.

Adding Movements to Out-of-Water Recovery

1. Clap hands.
2. Snap fingers.
3. Tap water with hand or fingers. This may be done on Back Crawl and Crawl strokes. As one arm finishes pull, tap water, then raise arm to overhead and begin pull. An additional variation is to do Back Crawl, cross arm over after pull, and tap water on other side before raising arm overhead for pull.
4. Cross arms on recovery. Do Double-Arm Backstroke and cross arms just above the surface after pull. Then open and bring them just above the surface to V position and repeat stroke.
5. Swish Crawl: On Crawl with head out, swish surface of the water with fingertips or the palm of the hand with the wrist bent, in recovery, while bringing the arm forward. The arm can be bent or straight.
6. Swish Spin/Turn: Execute a Swish but spin the body in the direction the arm is moving. The Swish Spin can stop at any point desired, such as quarter, half, three-quarter, or full circle.
7. Flying Breaststroke: Do Breaststroke and on glide raise arms just above surface and move them backward and then forward to glide position. Keep legs together while arms move backward and forward.

Changing Head Position

1. Use the head to complement the stroke by focusing on the hand and following it with the head.
2. Use sharp focus and head changes to contrast to the movement of the arms. The head position can change at any time during the stroke and can dramatically alter the effect of the stroke.

Changing the Tempo of the Stroke

1. Pauses: Substitute a pause for a stroke. The pause is usually done just after the recovery, but it could be added at any time during the stroking sequence. The pause is very effective because it is unexpected; during the pause is an excellent time to add head focus movements.
2. Double-time: Start stroking on a steady beat, then complete two strokes for every count, such as 1, 2, 3, and, 4, and.

Stroking movements for one person are usually viewed simply as transitions from one figure to another. So much more can be done with executed timing changes and expressive head, hand, and arm movements—additions that will make any solo composition more dynamic.

Sculling Variations

Sculling is essential for correctly executing a number of figures and their variations. Although the continued practice necessary to achieve sculling proficiency can be drudgery, there are many ways of working on sculling technique to make it interesting and fun while developing strength and finesse.

First, please read the material on sculling in chapters 2 and 20. More information on sculling and variations is in chapter 16.

Bent Knee Canoe: Do Canoe with one knee bent. This also may be done by bending both knees alternately.

Double-Bent Knee Canoe: Do Canoe and bend both knees, keeping toes at or above the surface.

Canoe Variation Sequence: Start with Canoe. Next do Bent Knee Canoe followed by Double-Bent Knee Canoe. Reverse the movements to finish in Canoe.

Bent Knee Torpedo: Start with Propeller Scull and assume Bent Knee position. This will cause the body to change from a horizontal to diagonal position, with the head down. Keep the body straight and

the foot of the straight leg at the surface. Experiment to discover ways of surfacing from this variation.

Ballet Leg Torpedo: Start with Propeller Scull and assume Ballet Leg position by bending one knee and extending the leg to vertical. This will cause the body to change from a horizontal to diagonal position, with the head down. Keep the body straight, with foot of the other leg at the surface. Experiment with different ways of surfacing.

Head-Out Periscope Variations: In these variations the head is out and the arms are forward just below the surface. Use Flat Scull to stay in place, Standard Scull to move backward, and Reverse Scull to move forward. First practice these variations while standing in shoulder depth water and then practice in deep water.

1. Body Vertical: Keep legs together and stretched.
2. Bent Knee: Same as body Vertical but one leg is in Bent Knee position. You may change the leg position while sculling, alternately bending one leg and then the other.

3. Vertical Ballet Leg: Perform Ballet Leg movements with the body Vertical.

4. Vertical Potpourri: With body Vertical, move the legs to different positions such as Bent Knee, L Split, Scissors Split, V Split, and so forth.

5. Vertical Tuck: From a Vertical position, tuck the body by drawing the knees toward the surface of the water and scull while in this position. Continue to scull while straightening the body back to Vertical.

6. Tub: Change from Vertical to Vertical Tuck, then roll back into standard Tub position and reverse.

Periscope Variations: In these variations the body is in an Inverted Vertical or Inverted Arched position. The legs should be above the surface at a constant level somewhere between the ankles and knees. Move the body backward at a constant speed by sculling.

Experiment with the position of the arms and the type of scull used to move the body backward in the water. In some cases, Bent Arm Flat Scull with arms overhead is effective. In other cases, Support Scull will be necessary. Try changing from one variation to the other. Also experiment with ways of surfacing after performing the variation.

1. Bent Knee Periscope: Perform Periscope with one knee bent and body straight.

2. Marching Periscope: Alternate bending knees while performing Bent Knee Periscope.

3. Arched Marching Periscope: Alternately bending knees while performing Periscope with the body arched.

4. Scissors Split Arched Periscope: Arch into a Scissors Split position and perform a Periscope. The legs may be reversed while doing this variation.

5. Inverted Tuck Periscope: Assume an Inverted Tuck position and perform Periscope.

6. Open Kneeling Periscope: Assume an inverted position in which the legs, from knees to toes, are on the surface of the water. Periscope in this position.

7. Scissors, V Split, Scissors: Assume an Inverted Arched-Scissors Split position and begin to Periscope. Move legs into a V Split position and then back to the Scissors Split. From the V Split position the legs can also be moved so that the forward leg in the first Scissors Split becomes the back leg in the second Scissors Split.

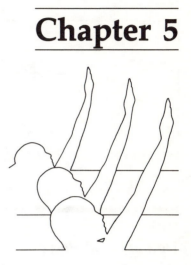

Chapter 5

Changing the Start, Middle, or End of Figures

Standard Figures always begin from the same starting position, follow the same movement sequence, and end the same way each time. But think of how many new, exciting, and unique movement combinations you can create by changing the start, middle, or end of the Standard Figures.

Changing the Start

Partial figures are frequently used to start and to finish variations. The following are only a small sample of the types of variations that can be created from any beginning position.

Dolphin Start (Figure 5.1):   The figure is started as a Dolphin, with the body either in a Boat or Back Layout position, to the point designated.

Figure 5.1. Dolphin Start

__Dolphin Into Kip__ (Figure 5.2):   Perform Dolphin to B. Tuck to Inverted Tuck (C) and straighten or thrust to Inverted Vertical (D). The Dolphin may be started with arms at the sides or overhead.

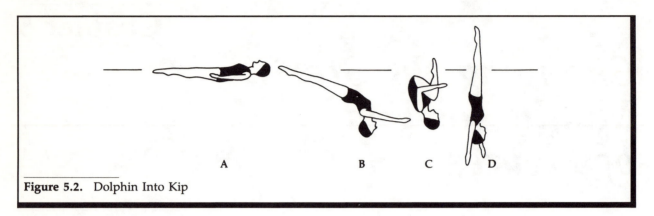

Figure 5.2.   Dolphin Into Kip

__Dolphin Into Porpoise__ (Figure 5.3):   A through C same as Dolphin into Kip. From C, straighten legs to horizontal so that body is in Inverted Pike (D). Raise legs to vertical as in Porpoise (E).

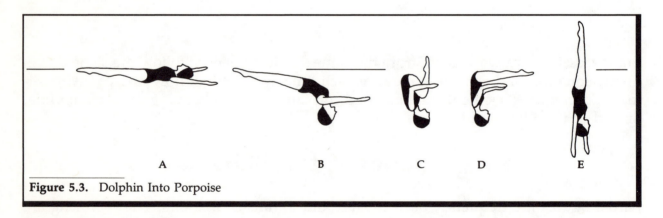

Figure 5.3.   Dolphin Into Porpoise

__The Albacore-Dolphin Roll Into Porpoise Variation__ (Figure 5.4):   A and B as Dolphin into Porpoise. *Keeping the feet at the surface,* make half roll (C) and pike so that the body is in Inverted Pike position (D). Raise one leg to vertical so that body is in Fishtail (E). Bend knee of horizontal leg (F) so that body is in Inverted Vertical Bent Knee position.

Figure 5.4.   The Albacore

Technique Tips

1. A Twist or Spin may be added to F.
2. Another position may be substituted for Fishtail (E).

**Spearfish to Fishtail** (Figure 5.5):   From Spearfish Ballet Leg (Flamingo) (A), tip backward to Inverted Spearfish (B). Raise horizontal leg to vertical and extend bent leg to horizontal so body is in Fishtail (C).

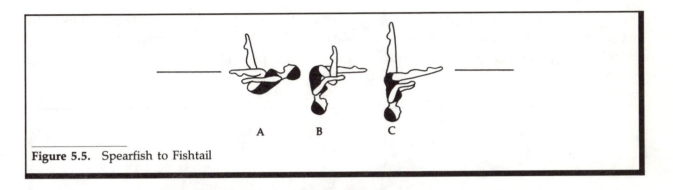

Figure 5.5.   Spearfish to Fishtail

Technique Tips

1. From B, the straight leg may remain horizontal, and the bent leg may be straightened to vertical.
2. Another Inverted Vertical position may be used instead of Fishtail.

**Backward Tuck to Fishtail** (Figure 5.6):   Do Backward Tuck Somersault to Inverted Tuck position. Open to Fishtail or Crane position.

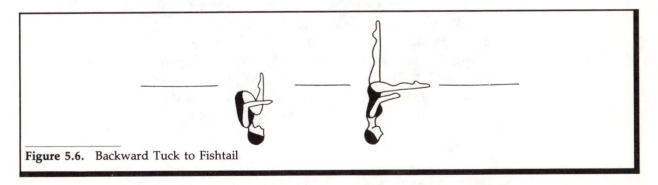

Figure 5.6.   Backward Tuck to Fishtail

**Backward Pike to Fishtail** (Figure 5.7):   Do Backward Pike Somersault to Inverted Pike position. Open to Fishtail or Crane position.

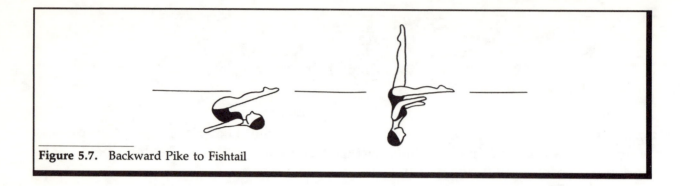

Figure 5.7. Backward Pike to Fishtail

**The Egret** (Figure 5.8):   From Ballet Leg position, r. leg vertical (A), arch as in Dolphin but keep r. leg vertical and submerge upper body (B). As body descends, bend l. knee, straightening body to Inverted Vertical Bent Knee position (C). Straighten l. leg to horizontal so that body is in Fishtail position (D).

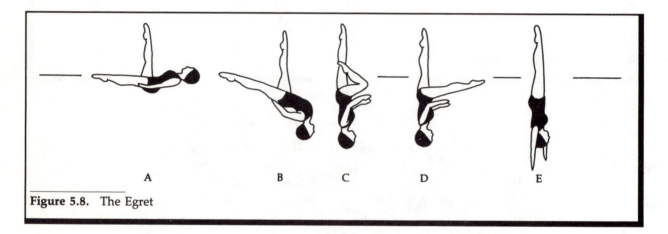

Figure 5.8. The Egret

Technique Tips

1. The Egret may be used as a means of assuming Inverted Vertical (position E) or Inverted Bent Knee position.
2. From Fishtail position you may twist as in Crane or raise l. leg to r. leg so that body is in Inverted Vertical position and submerge; Twist, Spin, or arch and finish as Foot-First Dolphin, and so on.

Changing the Middle Portion

**Multiple Kip** (Figure 5.9):   Perform Kip bending r. leg when in Inverted Vertical (D). Return to Inverted Tuck (E). Open to Inverted Vertical bending l. leg (F). Return to Inverted Tuck (G). Straighten to Inverted Vertical (H) and submerge. In this variation the middle portion is changed by repeating parts of the figure.

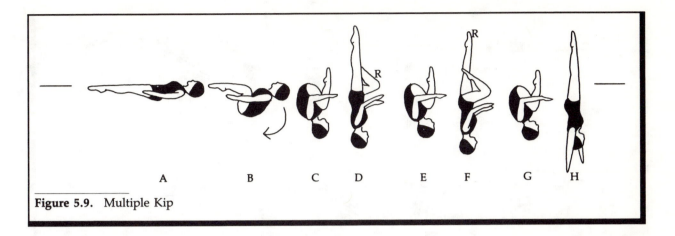

Figure 5.9.   Multiple Kip

Loop the Loop (Figure 5.10):   Start a Dolphin (A, B). At midway point somersault the body backward, keeping it arched (C), and finish as a regular Dolphin (D).

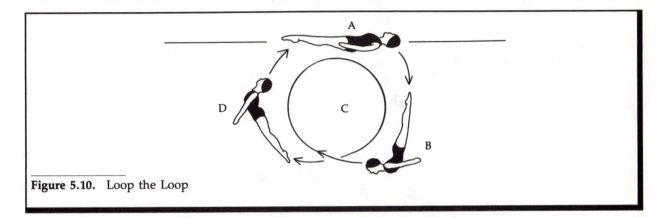

Figure 5.10.   Loop the Loop

Technique Tips

1. The body should be completely underwater throughout the arched somersault.
2. To somersault in an arched position, use the arms as you would in performing a Backward Pike Somersault, but with more power, and exert pressure toward the surface to keep the body from surfacing.
3. The somersault may be done in Tuck position instead of in Layout.

Walkover Somersault (Figure 5.11):   Do Forward Walkover to Scissors Split (C). Bend l. knee (D) and pike, somersaulting forward in Spearfish position (E) to F. Press r. leg up and over to water surface while arching (G) to finish as Swordfish (H). Right knee may be bent instead of l. knee.

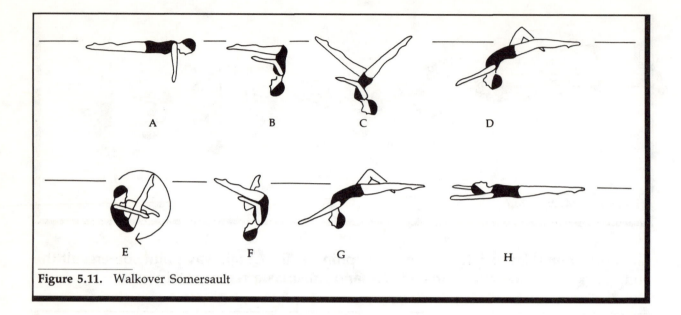

Figure 5.11.   Walkover Somersault

Finishing Figures and Changing the End

Finish as Dolphin (Figure 5.12):   The body is arched underwater, and a partial Dolphin is performed to surface the body, headfirst to Boat position.

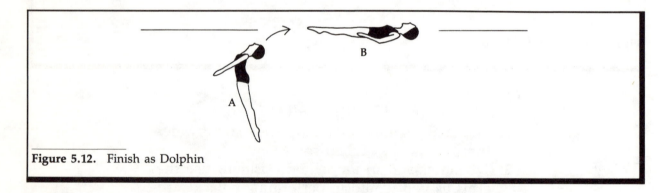

Figure 5.12.   Finish as Dolphin

Finish as Foot-First Dolphin (Figure 5.13):   From an Inverted position with the feet at the surface, the body is arched, and a partial Foot-First Dolphin is performed to surface the body feetfirst to a Back Layout position.

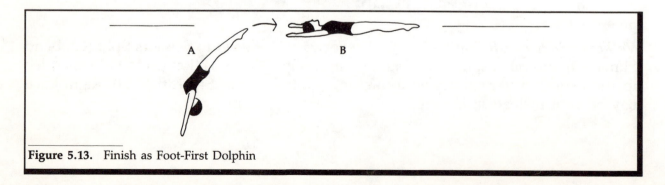

Figure 5.13.   Finish as Foot-First Dolphin

Finish as Swordfish (Figure 5.14):   From an Inverted Arched Bent Knee position, surface feetfirst to a Back Layout position. Straighten the bent leg as the body surfaces.

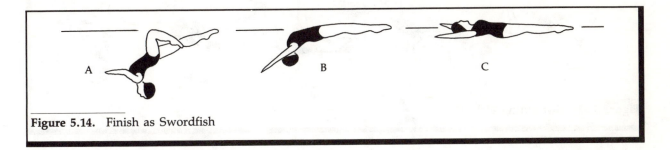

Figure 5.14. Finish as Swordfish

Finish as Forward Walkover (Figure 5.15):   When the body is in an Inverted Arched Scissors Split position, the forward leg is raised vertically overhead to the backward leg. Surface feetfirst to a Back Layout position.

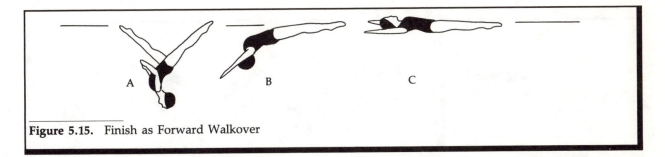

Figure 5.15. Finish as Forward Walkover

Finish as Backward Walkover (Figure 5.16):   From Inverted Arched Scissors Split position, raise the backward leg vertically overhead to the forward leg. Surface feetfirst to Front Layout position.

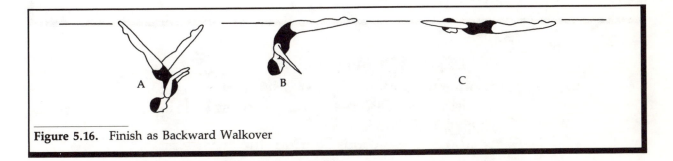

Figure 5.16. Finish as Backward Walkover

Swordfish Catalina (Figure 5.17):   Do Swordfish to C. When in C, straighten bent leg to vertical, body to horizontal and rise in Ballet Leg Sub (D). Just before head surfaces, do Catalina (E) to Fishtail (F). Submerge headfirst in Inverted Vertical. Raise horizontal leg to Vertical to assume Inverted Vertical position. A Catalina or Eiffel Tower variation may also be used.

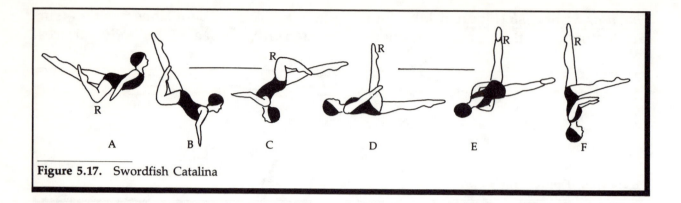

Figure 5.17. Swordfish Catalina

Foot-First Spin Walk-Up (Figure 5.18):   Start Bent Knee Foot-First Dolphin (A, B) and continue until straight leg is vertical on ascent. Straighten body to Inverted Vertical (C), rising as high as possible feetfirst. At the highest point, do half spin, opening legs to Scissors Split (D). Finish as Forward Walkover (E) to Front Layout.

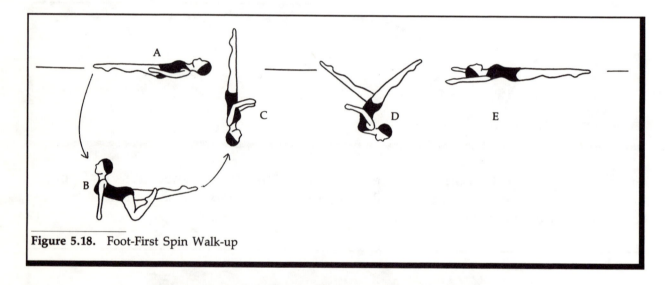

Figure 5.18.   Foot-First Spin Walk-up

Technique Tips

1. Foot-First Dolphin may be started with arms at the sides in Reverse Scull or overhead in Propeller (Torpedo).
2. Scull or use scoops during the Foot-First Dolphin.
3. Eliminate the spin. D and E will then be done moving in the opposite direction to that shown in Figure 5.18.

Chapter 6

Arm and Leg Variations

The arms and legs can be the most visible and expressive parts of the body when performing aquatic movements. By using arms and legs in unexpected or unique ways, variations can be developed that can make even the simplest movements more effective.

Ballet Leg Variations

Ballet Leg March (Figure 6.1):   From Boat (A), assume Sailboat position, r. leg bent (B). Exchange position of legs so that left is bent (C). Straighten l. leg to vertical so that body is in Ballet Leg position (D). Lower l. leg to surface, keeping it straight, and finish in Boat (E). Repeat, bending l. leg at start.

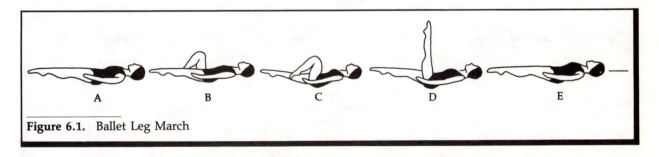

Figure 6.1. Ballet Leg March

Ballet Leg With Side Bend Finish (Figure 6.2):   From Boat (A), assume Sailboat position, r. leg bent (B). Extend r. leg to vertical (C). Bend r. leg and at the same time twist the body to the left from the waist so that the bent leg touches the surface of the water (D). Straighten r. leg to horizontal and at the same time return the hips to horizontal so that body is in Boat (E). Repeat with other leg.

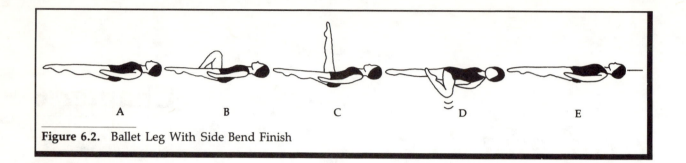

Figure 6.2. Ballet Leg With Side Bend Finish

**Rond de Jambe Ballet Leg** (Figure 6.3):   From Boat (A), assume Sailboat position, r. leg bent (B), and raise leg to half-extended position shown in C. Make a circle with the foot, rotating the leg from the knee, similar to rond de jambe in ballet but without the turn-out. Extend r. leg to vertical so that body is in Ballet Leg position (D). Lower r. leg, keeping it straight, to finish in Boat (E).

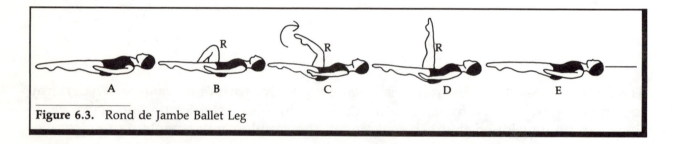

Figure 6.3. Rond de Jambe Ballet Leg

Technique Tips

1. Keep thigh in place while doing rond de jambe movement.
2. You may make a circle inward or outward.
3. If you wish, you may touch the surface of the water with the toes on the lowest part of the circular movement.

**V Split Crisscross** (Figure 6.4):   From Double Ballet Leg Position, open legs to V Split (A). Close legs, crossing them with r. leg forward (B). Exchange position so that l. leg is forward (C). Repeat.

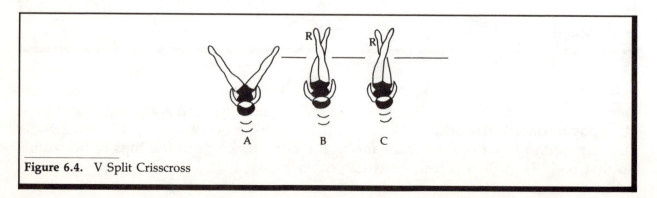

Figure 6.4. V Split Crisscross

Technique Tip

1. Turn out the legs from the hips when doing this variation.

Foot-to-Hand Ballet Leg (Figure 6.5):   Perform Back Crawl. When r. arm is overhead (A), kick r. leg up with knee straight and at the same time bring r. arm vertically forward to touch foot (B). Lower leg to surface and return arm to overhead position (C), continuing Back Crawl. Repeat, using l. leg and arm.

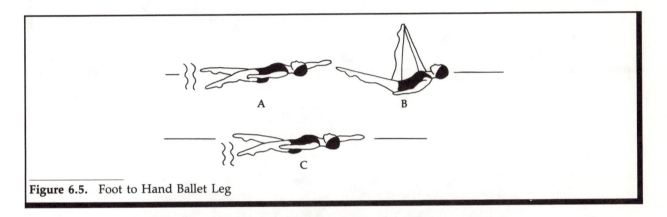

Figure 6.5.   Foot to Hand Ballet Leg

Technique Tips

1. Do several strokes to gain momentum and to help propel and support the body in B before performing the variation.
2. As soon as l. arm completes pull to side as in A, begin sculling with it to aid in supporting and propelling the body.
3. The hand-and-foot connection may be made in a variety of ways, such as the palm touching front of foot, front of ankle, or side of foot or ankle, or using the back of the hand.
4. The effect is neater if the legs are closed a moment just prior to raising one leg and again after lowering leg but before resuming Flutter Kick.

Crossover (Figure 6.6):   The same as in Foot-to-Hand Ballet Leg but the hand of the opposite arm touches raised foot.

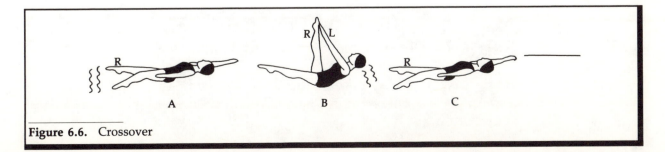

Figure 6.6.   Crossover

Sub Variation (Figure 6.7): Do Foot-to-Hand Ballet Leg or Crossover variation but keep hand to foot and sink as in Sub.

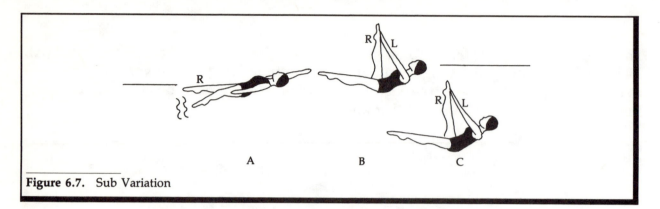

Figure 6.7. Sub Variation

Technique Tips

1. By overextending raised leg and letting body tip backward while submerging, you can go into a Backward Somersault movement.
2. By letting the body tip forward when submerging, you can go into a Forward Somersault movement.
3. Bend the knee of horizontal leg when submerging.

Foot-to-Hand Into Scissors Split (Figure 6.8): Start in Back Layout, arms in V (A). Raise one leg overhead and at the same time pike and bring one arm forward so that hand and part of arm are out of the water, head and trunk are below surface (B). Arch to Inverted position with legs in Scissors Split (C).

Figure 6.8. Foot-to-Hand Into Scissors Split

Technique Tips

1. From A, both arms may be raised and touch foot in B.
2. From B, you may pike or tuck and do partial or complete Somersault in Tuck, Pike, or Spearfish position.

3. The hand is in contact with the foot only at the start of the movement, and then it is used as usual for arching or somersaulting movements.

Arm Variations in Tuck and Pike Positions

**One-Arm Tuck** (Figure 6.9):   Start in Back Layout, arms in V (A). Tuck and raise one arm up vertically so that hand is out of the water (B). Somersault backward. The same may be done in Spearfish position instead of tuck.

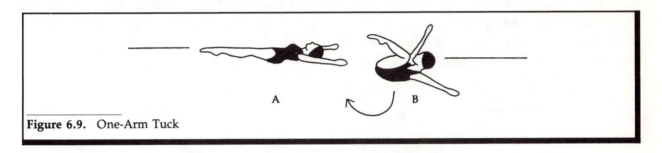

Figure 6.9.   One-Arm Tuck

**Tuck Through Arms** (Figure 6.10):   When on back, raise arms overhead to V (A). Tuck body and somersault backward through the raised arms (B).

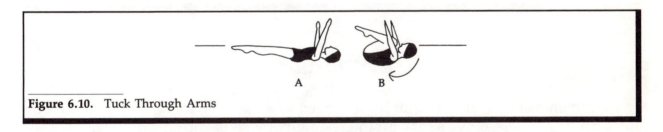

Figure 6.10.   Tuck Through Arms

Technique Tips

1. Start from a stroke, raising arms either from sides or from overhead to vertical.
2. Close legs just prior to Somersault.
3. Only the first part of the Somersault is done through the raised arms. As the body somersaults, the arms also change positions and can be used as in a usual Somersault to complete the figure.

**One-Arm Dolphin Somersault** (Figure 6.11):   When on the back, raise r. arm to vertical (A). Arch, bending r. leg and keeping r. arm vertical, and submerge upper body as if starting Dolphin (B). At this point (B), bend knee of other leg and pike body, somersaulting backward in this position (C). This variation may be started from a stroke.

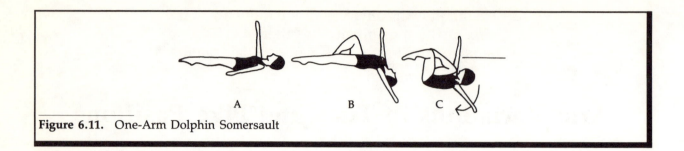

Figure 6.11. One-Arm Dolphin Somersault

Forward Pike, Arm Out (Figure 6.12):   Sidestroke or do Flutter Kick on side, and when in Sidestroke glide (A), roll onto front and pike, lifting arm that was on top when on side above the surface to vertical (B). The momentum from the kick and other arm starts the body piking. As upper body submerges, the raised arm moves into position for movements to follow. From C, somersault forward or straighten to Inverted Vertical. Experiment with starting figures, raising one or both arms above the surface, to discover additional variations.

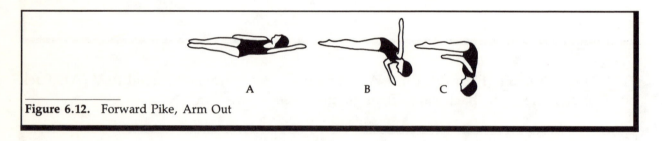

Figure 6.12. Forward Pike, Arm Out

Exchanges

In movements of this type, an arm is exchanged to a leg, a leg for an arm, or both arms for both legs. These movements are interesting because of the surprise element. The viewer sees the body submerge with a leg raised and assumes the leg will emerge as the body surfaces, but an exchange is made underwater so that an arm emerges.

Exchanging a Leg for an Arm (Figure 6.13):   From a position on the side, kick and raise up top arm so that body is in a vertical or near vertical position (A). Sink in this position. While sinking, pike underwater, keeping arm vertical (B). When hand has submerged, bring one leg up to vertical, bending the other to the chest so that the body is in the Spearfish (Flamingo) Sub position (C). Rise to the surface in this position (D).

Technique Tip

1. By piking as the body submerges, the exchange can be made quicker than if the body is kept straight until entirely submerged. Therefore, if you wish to lengthen the time underwater, do not pike until the body has completely submerged.

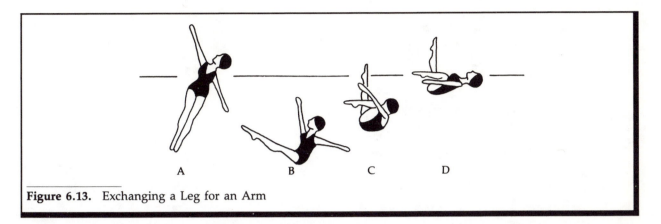

Figure 6.13. Exchanging a Leg for an Arm

Exchanging an Arm for a Leg (Figure 6.14): From an Inverted Vertical position (A), submerge, do a pike to Vertical (B), but rise to surface with one arm extended overhead (C).

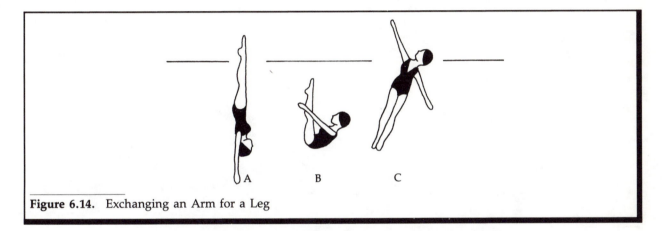

Figure 6.14. Exchanging an Arm for a Leg

Technique Tips

1. You may tuck instead of pike to Vertical.
2. In opening from tuck or pike to Vertical, a kick will speed the surfacing of the body and will also bring it out higher than otherwise, although you may float up if you wish to rise slowly.
3. You may rise with both arms extended overhead, in a V, or in another position.
4. To lengthen the time underwater, completely submerge in Inverted Vertical before piking or tucking to Vertical.

Pike-Up, Walk-Through, and Roll Variations

Chapter 7

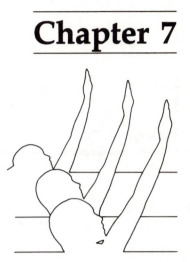

The Pike-Up, Walk-Through, and Roll variations described in this chapter demonstrate effective methods of ending figures in different ways, adding leg movements in the middle of figures, and adding body rolls to create unique variations.

The Pike-Up is not only a different way to get into a Vertical position from an Inverted Vertical position but also a good habit to adopt for ending Standard Figures. When practicing Standard Figures, swimmers will often arch out of an Inverted Vertical to get back to the surface. Anticipating this arch can make it difficult to achieve a good Inverted Vertical position. By using a Pike-Up described in the following section, you can end figures in a way that will not affect an Inverted Vertical position and will in fact give you a little added Vertical position practice on the way to the surface.

Pike-Ups

In Pike-Up variations (Figure 7.1), the figure is completed by piking the body to Vertical position as follows:

From Inverted Vertical (A), pike, keeping legs vertical (B). Open body to Vertical as it rises (using the buoyancy of the body) and raise the arms to T position so that the body is vertical as the head surfaces and the arms are in T position (C). The Pike-Up may be added to any figure variation in which the body submerges in an Inverted Vertical position (Porpoise, Catalina, Eiffel Tower, etc.).

Figure 7.1. The Pike-Up

Technique Tips

1. Bend the head forward to initiate the piking of the body.
2. Raising the arms to the T position at the finish should be done smoothly and evenly. The top surface of the arms, as they are raised, will slow the ascent of the body so it doesn't pop out.
3. When done correctly, there is a floating feeling to the movements. The body changes position gracefully and with very little effort.

The Thrust-Up

The Thrust-Up (Figure 7.2) is a powerful movement that allows the body to achieve maximum height and lift. From a pike position with the legs pointed to the surface of the water (A), scull the body upwards until the head almost reaches the surface. Press down with the back and arms while straightening the body to an Inverted Vertical and catch to Support Scull (C). You may keep your legs together, have one knee bent, or go into another position such as a split.

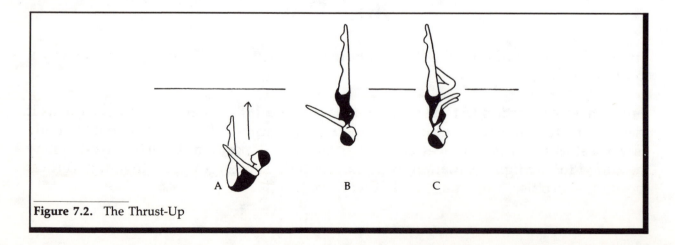

Figure 7.2. The Thrust-Up

Walk-Through Variations

The Cero–Fishtail Walk-Through Thrust (Figure 7.3):   Porpoise to Fishtail (C), r. leg horizontal. Bend r. leg and move it backward while bringing l. leg forward (D) and begin piking body. Continue the leg movements so the r. leg straightens to vertical, the l. leg bends, and the body is in Spearfish Sub (F). Rise. Just before the head surfaces, thrust to Inverted Vertical (G), and submerge headfirst.

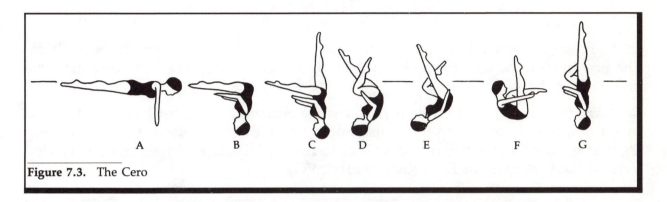

Figure 7.3. The Cero

Technique Tips

1. Move the legs as if walking or pedaling backward.
2. You may omit F and G and finish by surfacing to Spearfish Ballet Leg position.

The Snook–Walk-Through to Fishtail (Figure 7.4):   From Ballet Leg position, r. leg vertical (A), arch as in start of Dolphin but bend r. leg (B). Pike, raising l. leg up and forward as r. knee bend increases (C), and Walk-Through to Fishtail (D). Without pausing in D, bend l. leg so body is in Inverted Vertical Bent Knee position (E). Straighten l. leg to Inverted Vertical and submerge (F).

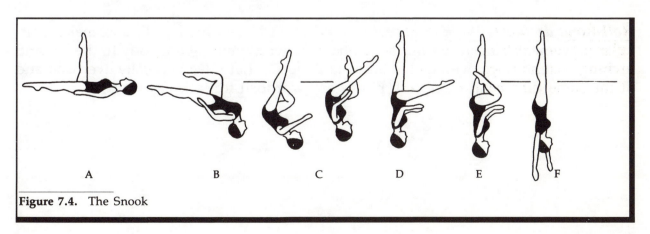

Figure 7.4. The Snook

Rolls

In the following variations, half rolls are used with the body in a Bent Knee position. The first roll is done with the body horizontal, the second with the body on a diagonal line. Roll in the same direction.

Roll Kip (Figure 7.5):   From Boat (A), assume Sailboat, r. leg bent (B). Do half roll to left into Bent Knee Canoe (C). Raise upper body, then sink so that foot of straight leg is at surface (D). Do half roll to E. Tuck to Inverted Tuck (F). Straighten to Inverted Vertical (legs together or Bent Knee position)(G).

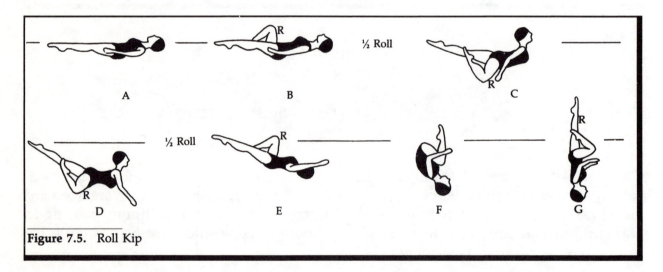

Figure 7.5.   Roll Kip

Roll-Rond de Jambe Walk (Figure 7.6):   When in E, bend r. leg (F) and make a circular movement (similar to rond de jambe in ballet); while rolling body to the left and arching, extend r. leg overhead to Scissors Split (G). Lift l. leg vertically overhead and at the same time bend r. leg (H). Finish as Swordfish to Back Layout (I).

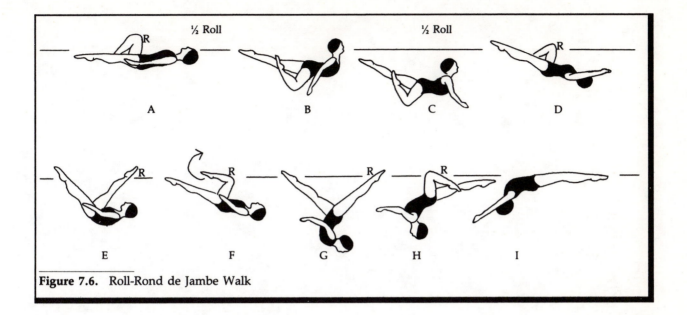

Figure 7.6. Roll-Rond de Jambe Walk

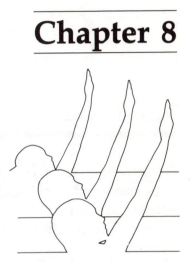

Chapter 8

Gymnastic and Tap Figures

You don't have to be a gymnast to perform gymnastic figures in the water. In fact, some of the Standard Figures you are already familiar with, such as Somersaults, are themselves gymnastic. However, you may have overlooked the pool bottom as an aid in performing new variations, practicing positions, and adapting land movements to the water. Gymnastic movements are easily transferred to the water by using the bottom.

Be especially careful not to hit your head on the bottom when performing any movements in shallow water. Keep the hands above the head on headfirst descents so that the hands will contact the bottom first.

Forward Springing Figures

Start all the figures described in the following section from a standing position in waist-deep to shoulder-deep water. Spring, piking the body and bringing the head forward, arms over the head, almost as if you were diving and wanted to enter the water near the side of the pool. Bend the wrists so that the palms make contact with the bottom, with arms separated about shoulder width. Bend the elbows somewhat as the palms contact the bottom to absorb the force of the ''dive'' and to aid in balance. From this Inverted Pike position you can do a variety of movements.

Handstand Somersault (Figure 8.1):   From a standing position (A), spring to Inverted Pike (B). Raise one leg to vertical (C). Raise other leg to vertical so body is in a handstand position (D). Hold. Bend elbows, then straighten while pushing from bottom with palms to raise the body feetfirst as high as possible. Quickly tuck (E) and do a partial Backward Somersault. Finish in Standing position (F).

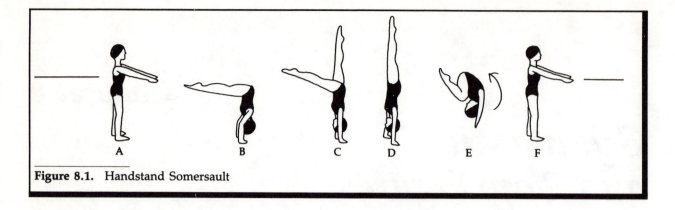

Figure 8.1. Handstand Somersault

Handstand Walkover Variation (Figure 8.2):   Spring to Inverted Vertical (B). Raise l. leg overhead, arching into Scissors Split (C). Bend r. knee and push from bottom with hands (D). Finish as Swordfish to Back Layout (E). An additional variation is to finish in Standing position instead of Back Layout.

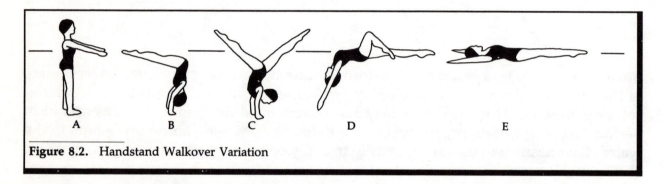

Figure 8.2. Handstand Walkover Variation

Forward Round-Off (Figure 8.3):   From Handstand position (C), make half pivot on palms (D). Push from the bottom with hands, and when body is at the highest point, quickly pike, slapping water with front surface of legs (E). Tuck (F) and do partial Backward Somersault to Standing position.

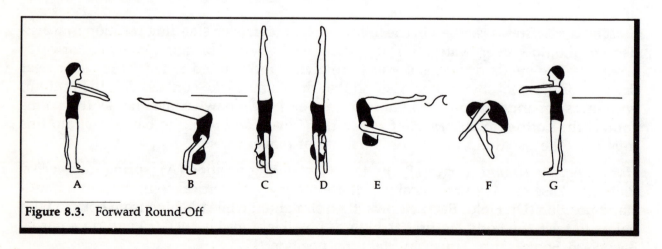

Figure 8.3. Forward Round-Off

Backward Springing Figures

Do these figures in chest-deep to shoulder-deep water and, if necessary, use a small pull with one hand to get the body Inverted so that the other hand makes contact with the bottom first. Be very careful not to hit the head or face on the bottom.

Backward Handspring (Figure 8.4):   From Standing position (A), spring backward, arching as much as possible, keeping the head backward and arms overhead (B). Bend wrists so the palms make contact with bottom and also bend elbows slightly to help absorb the shock. Straighten to Handstand position (C). Push from bottom with hands, piking body so front of legs hits water surface (D). Tuck and do partial Backward Somersault (E) to Standing position (F). This figure may be done without pausing, or you may pause briefly in C.

Figure 8.4.   Backward Handspring

Backward Spring Tuck (Figure 8.5):   Spring backward into a Handstand position (C). Hold. Bend elbows and push from bottom with hands so body rises feetfirst as high as possible. At height of rise, quickly tuck (D) and do Backward Somersault to Standing position (E).

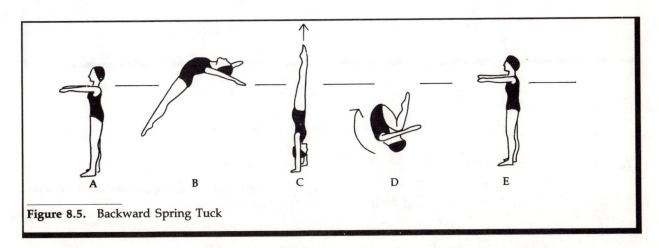

Figure 8.5.   Backward Spring Tuck

Backward Round-Off (Figure 8.6):   Spring backward to Handstand position (C). Make half turn (pivot on hands) to D. Push from the bottom with hands and quickly pike when body is at its highest point, slapping water with front surface of legs (E). Tuck (F) and do partial Somersault to Standing position (G). Another variation is to finish as a Backward Walkover to Front Layout from E.

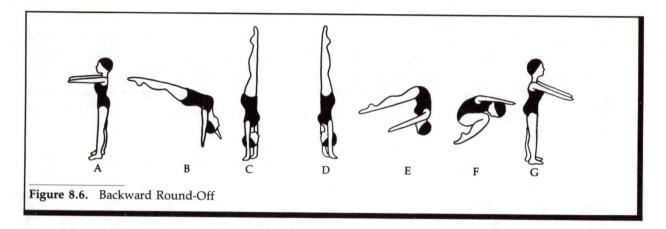

Figure 8.6.   Backward Round-Off

Gym Potpourri (Figure 8.7):   When in Handstand position, change to one or more of the illustrated positions. Either return to Handstand position after each one or flow from one position to another. Start, finish, and vary the order as you wish. You can balance on one hand instead of both hands in some positions.

Figure 8.7.   Gym Potpourri

Fun With Tap Figures

Tap dancing in the water? Why not! Of course, like any other land activity that is taken into the water, adaptations have to be made to translate it into an aquatic movement. The following tap figures should help you invent many more.

Ballet Leg Tap (Figure 8.8):   From Boat (A), bend r. leg (B). Straighten to vertical (C). Bend r. leg again, crossing it over l. leg so r. foot taps water on l. side of l. leg (D). Raise r. leg to vertical (E). Bend r. leg and tap water with foot on r. side of l. leg (F). Straighten to horizontal (G). Repeat using the other leg. Travel while doing this variation.

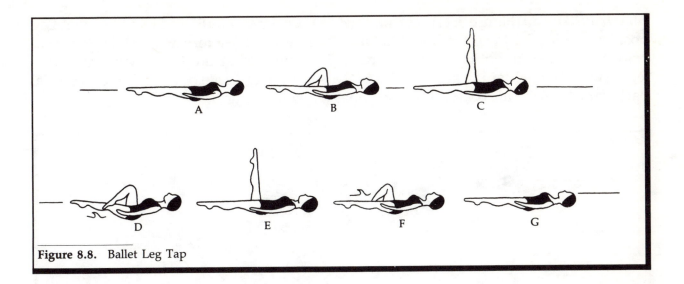

Figure 8.8. Ballet Leg Tap

**Forward Walkover Tap Variation** (Figure 8.9): Do Forward Walkover to Scissors Split (C). Bend forward leg so that foot taps water surface (D). Return to Scissors Split (E). Finish as Forward Walkover. Additional variation from E: Raise forward leg overhead (knee straight) and at the same time bend knee of other leg, bringing it forward. Finish as Swordfish.

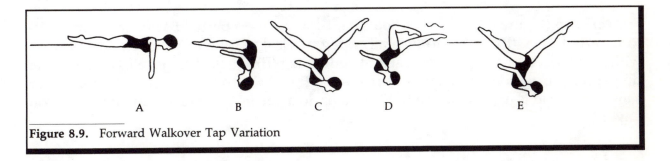

Figure 8.9. Forward Walkover Tap Variation

**Backward Walkover Tap Variation** (Figure 8.10): From Boat (A), arch upper body as in start of Dolphin but bend r. knee (B). Extend r. leg overhead to Scissors Split (C). Bend r. leg so foot taps surface (D). Straighten r. leg forward (E). Bend l. leg, piking body and keeping r. foot at surface (F). Surface feetfirst, straightening l. leg, to finish in Front Layout (G) (H).

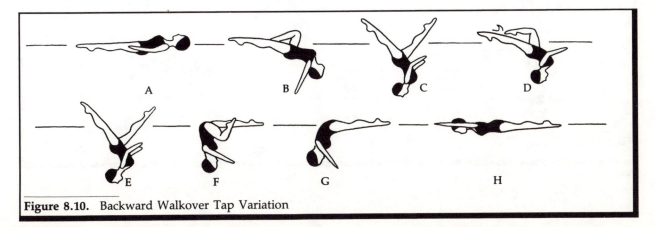

Figure 8.10. Backward Walkover Tap Variation

Inverted Pike Tap (Figure 8.11):   From Boat (A), assume Tub (B) and Double Ballet Leg position (C). Tip backward to Inverted Pike (D). Keeping l. leg forward, bend r. leg backward from knee so foot taps water in back (E). Body arches on this movement. Lift r. leg forward, straightening knee so that body is in Inverted Pike (F). Tuck and do partial Backward Somersault (G,H). Open to Boat (I) or to Vertical.

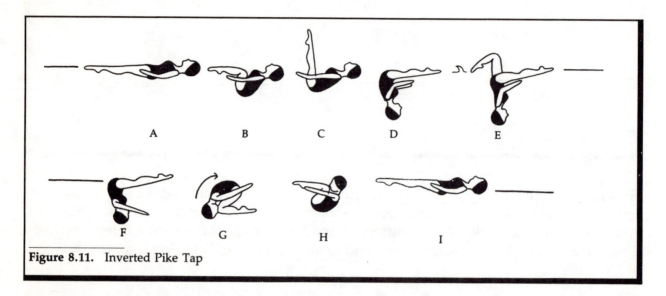

Figure 8.11.   Inverted Pike Tap

Fishtail Tap (Figure 8.12):   From Boat (A), tuck, then do partial Backward Somersault to Inverted Tuck (B). Open to Fishtail, r. leg vertical (C). Bend r. knee and tap water with foot (D). Raise r. leg to vertical and bend l. leg (E). Tuck to Inverted Tuck (F), then do partial Backward Somersault to surface (G, H). Open to Boat (I) or continue Somersault until head is up, then open to Vertical or do a partial Somersault and open to Front Layout.

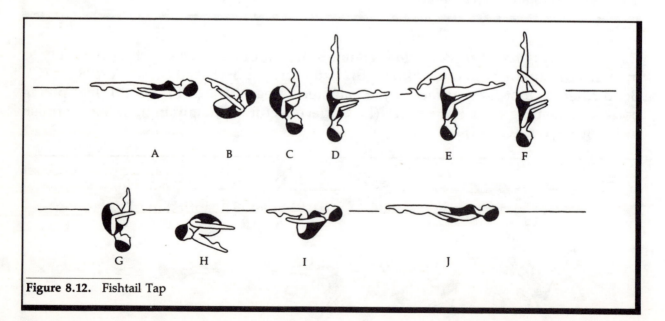

Figure 8.12.   Fishtail Tap

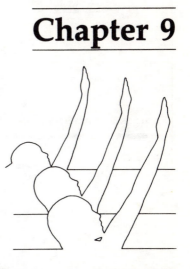

Chapter 9

Add-On Variations

By taking a figure or part of a figure and adding on another figure or part of another figure, you can make a great many variations. This chapter contains some examples.

Shark-Dolphin-Shark-SDS (Figure 9.1):   Do a Bent Knee Shark, making a circle at the surface (A). Without pausing, roll onto the back and go into a Bent Knee Dolphin (B). As the body nears the surface, again do a quarter roll, this time onto the other side, and perform Bent Knee Shark (C), making a complete circle. Extend one arm overhead for the Shark before the head surfaces in the Dolphin.

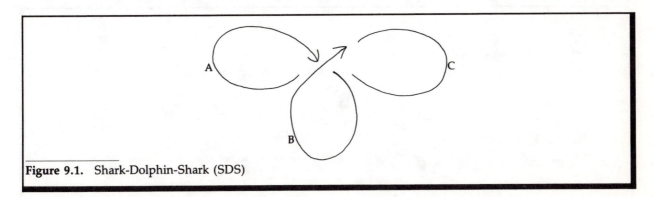

Figure 9.1.   Shark-Dolphin-Shark (SDS)

Somersub Catalina (Figure 9.2):   Perform Somersub to Double Ballet Leg Sub position (C). Rise in Sub, lowering l. leg to horizontal so that body is in Ballet Leg position just below surface (D). Rise and do Catalina (E, F). Submerge headfirst in Inverted Vertical.

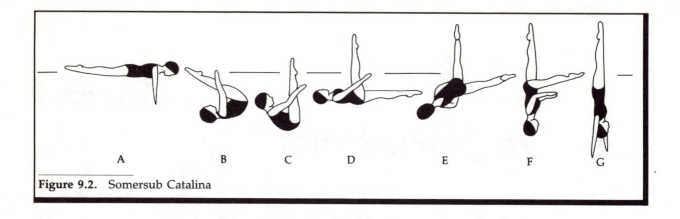

Figure 9.2. Somersub Catalina

Technique Tips

1. When in C, the single Ballet Leg position may be assumed before rising toward surface, instead of while rising.
2. A Catalina variation may be used instead of the Standard Figure.
3. From D, do Eiffel Tower or Eiffel Tower variation.

Dolphin-Somersault-Kip-DSK (Figure 9.3): This variation was originated by Jackie Brayshaw of England. Do a Dolphin to halfway point (B). Quickly tuck (C) and do Backward Somersault to Inverted Tuck (D). Thrust to Inverted Vertical as in Kip (E).

Figure 9.3. Dolphin Somersault Kip (DSK)

Technique Tips

1. There is a nice contrast of movement in this variation. The Dolphin part is performed slowly and smoothly. The tucking is a quick contraction of the body, and the extension to Inverted Vertical is a thrusting movement.
2. Let the body rise to the surface as the Somersault is being executed.

The PS (Figure 9.4):   This figure variation was originated by Peg Seller of Canada. Do a Porpoise to Fishtail, r. leg horizontal (C). Bend r. knee so that body is in Inverted Vertical Bent Knee position (D). Tuck and do Backward Somersault (E) to Inverted Tuck (F). Straighten to Inverted Vertical (G), immediately open legs into Scissor Split, and arch body (H). Finish as Forward Walkover (I, J).

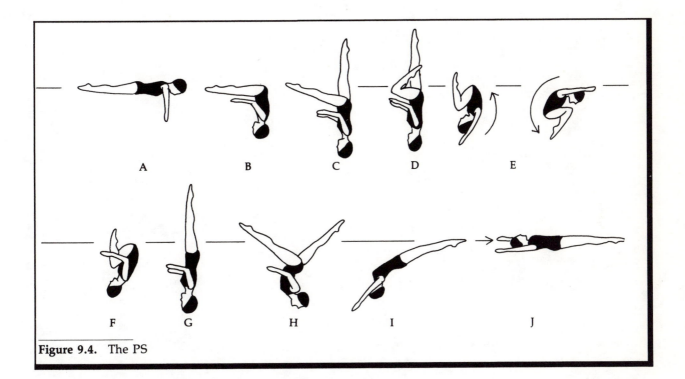

Figure 9.4. The PS

Chapter 10

Twist, Swivel, Swirl, and Spin Variations

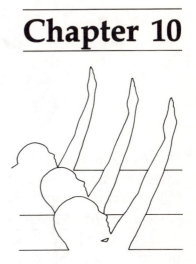

The movements of Twist, Swivel, Swirl, and Spin at first glance appear to be similar, but they are really quite different. A descriptive definition of each will be helpful both for learning to perform these movements and for explaining their differences and similarities.

Twist: The body rotates in a Vertical or Inverted Vertical position to the right or left. The level of the body in the water remains constant, and the body turns in place without traveling. Twists may be performed either with the head or feet out of the water or with the entire body under the surface.

Swivel: A Swivel is a Twist variation that is performed in an Inverted Vertical position with the knees bent so that the legs (from knees to toes) are horizontal and turn at the surface of the water (Inverted Kneel).

Swirl: A Swirl refers to movements in which the legs change from a Scissors Split (with one leg forward) to a V Split, then to a Scissors Split (with the other leg forward). It can be performed in Inverted Vertical or in a Pike position with the back parallel to the bottom.

Spin: A Spin is a Twist performed while the body is rising or descending.

You may execute these movements in several positions. In the Vertical position, the head is out, the arms just below the surface. Inverted positions include Inverted Tuck, Inverted Kneel, Inverted Open Kneel, Inverted Vertical, Inverted Vertical Bent Knee, Fishtail, Inverted Vertical V Split, and Inverted Vertical Scissors Split. Assume these positions in any manner you prefer and then execute the Twist, Swivel, Swirl, or Spin variations.

The Shuttle (Figure 10.1):   When in Inverted Vertical, make approximately one-quarter twist, first in one direction and then in the opposite direction. Repeat.

> **Technique Tips**
> 1. Use only one movement of the arms for each Twist.
> 2. Make certain that the body is in balance before starting to twist.
> 3. Keep back straight, head in line with the body.

V Split Crisscross Twist (Figure 10.2):   From Inverted V Split, open legs to V Split (A). Twist, crossing legs with r. leg in front (B), and exchange position so l. leg is in front (C). Open to V Split and repeat.

Scissors Split Crisscross (Figure 10.3):   Same as a V Split Crisscross, but substitute Scissors Split for V Split. Straighten the back and bring head in line with the body when not in Scissors Split.

Bent-Knee Change (Figure 10.4):   While twisting, bend l. knee (A), straighten (B), bend r. knee (C), straighten. Continue to twist while changing positions. Another variation is to start with the l. leg bent (A) and, while twisting, to exchange position of legs (C). Omit B.

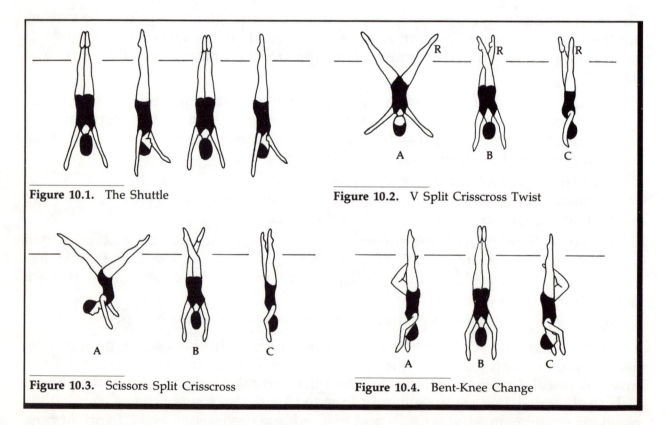

Figure 10.1. The Shuttle

Figure 10.2. V Split Crisscross Twist

Figure 10.3. Scissors Split Crisscross

Figure 10.4. Bent-Knee Change

Inverted Kneel to Bent Knee (Figure 10.5):   Perform at least half Twist in Inverted Kneel position (A). Straighten one leg to vertical while continuing to twist (B), then perform at least another half Twist in this position.

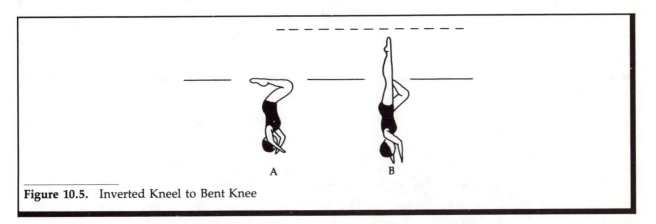

Figure 10.5. Inverted Kneel to Bent Knee

Pompano (Figure 10.6):   Perform Porpoise to Inverted Vertical (C) and immediately arch, bending knees to Inverted Open Kneel (D). Do a full Twist (E). Tuck to Inverted Tuck (F) and do a full Twist (G). Thrust to Inverted Vertical Bent Knee (H), and submerge headfirst.

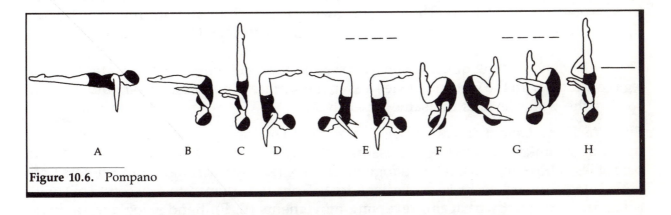

Figure 10.6. Pompano

Technique Tips

1. This variation offers opportunity to vary rhythm and quality of movement.
2. From C, the knees may be bent sharply so that backs of legs (from knees to toes) slap surface.
3. Half Twists may be used instead of full Twists.

Swivel (Figure 10.7):   Assume an Inverted Kneel position (A). Keeping legs from feet to knees at surface, tuck and roll. Start by using an Inward Pull with one arm, followed by an Outward Press toward the surface with the other. Open the bend of the body at the hips so that the trunk changes from horizontal to diagonal, to inverted, to diagonal, and back to horizontal. Repeat.

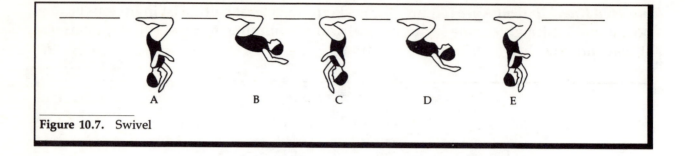

Figure 10.7. Swivel

Technique Tips

1. Part of the momentum for the Swivel comes from the action of changing the angle at the hips during the movements.
2. If pressure is not exerted toward the surface on the outward press, you can swivel up to the surface using a Marlin type of movement.

Swirl: A Swirl is executed with the legs as they change position from a Scissors Split with the r. leg forward to a Scissors Split with the l. leg forward. To get the idea, practice it first using the arms instead of the legs: Stand and raise the arms overhead, open to Scissors Split with the r. arm forward, swing to a V Split and around to a Scissors Split so that the r. arm is backward. The movements may also be reversed.

The Swirl may be done quickly, slowly, or at a moderate tempo. Keep water level on legs constant, with the feet and ankles above the surface. Split positions should be even, so that the water level is the same on each leg.

Swirl to Front Layout (Figure 10.8):   From Boat (A), raise l. leg overhead, piking so upper body sinks and legs are in Scissors Split (B). Keeping body piked, with feet and part of legs above the surface, exchange position of legs by Swirling. From Scissors Split with l. leg forward as in B, move legs to V Split (C), then into Scissors Split with r. leg forward (D). Swirl again, reversing movements (E, F). Bend r. leg and tip backward (G). Use Front Scoop to surface body feetfirst, straightening bent leg, to finish in Front Layout (H). Note that in Swirl, each foot makes a half circle on a horizontal plane.

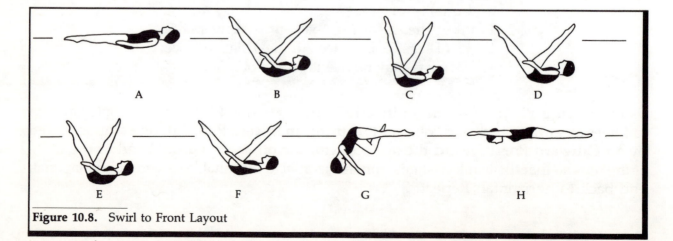

Figure 10.8. Swirl to Front Layout

Swirl Spearfish Kip (Figure 10.9): A through F same as in Swirl to Front Layout. From F, bend backward leg, bringing it forward to chest so that the body tips backward to Inverted Spearfish position (G). Straighten to Inverted Vertical, raising l. leg and keeping r. leg bent (H). Submerge headfirst either in Bent Knee position or with legs together.

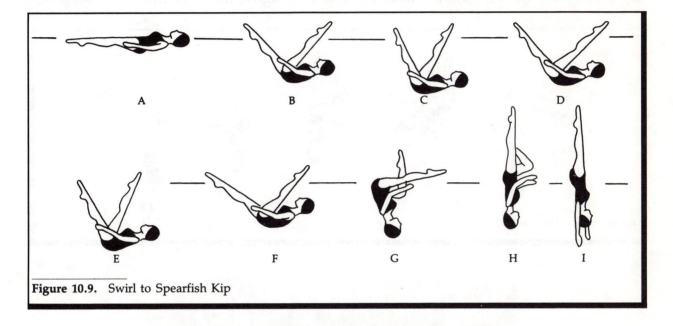

Figure 10.9. Swirl to Spearfish Kip

Technique Tips

1. Get as much height as possible on H.
2. In changing from G to Inverted Vertical Bent Knee position, you may raise r. leg to vertical and bend l. leg, instead of as shown above, or both legs may be extended to vertical.

Cat Spin (Figure 10.10): Assume Ballet Leg position, r. leg vertical (A). Perform Catalina (B) to Fishtail (C). Bend l. leg (D). Spin while straightening l. leg to vertical (E) and submerge (F). Perform smoothly with constant speed of movement.

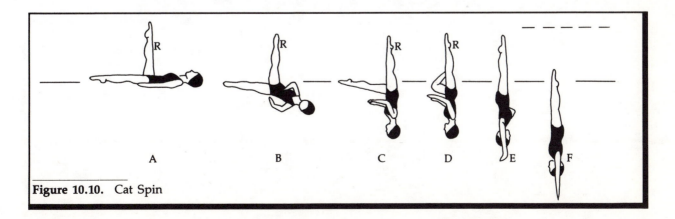

Figure 10.10. Cat Spin

The Eagle (Figure 10.11):   From Double Ballet Leg position (A), bend r. leg to a right-angle position while doing Catalina roll-change (B) so that when body is in Inverted Vertical, the r. leg is still in a right-angle bend position (C). Without pausing, continue to turn in the same direction using a Spin and bringing r. leg to Bent Knee position (D). Submerge while spinning. The r. leg may be straightened to vertical on the descent.

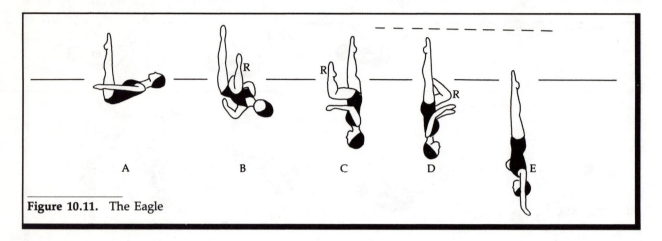

Figure 10.11.   The Eagle

Chapter 11

Suspension Figures

Because the water gives some support to the body, it is possible to float in a number of different positions, to change position, and to achieve the feeling of weightlessness. The ability to do these figures is dependent on buoyancy, balance, and control.

Balance is achieved and maintained in suspension figures primarily through positioning the parts of the body in correct alignment so that the body is suspended in a particular position. A position is usually changed by stretching, contracting, rolling, or using a pendulum type of movement. A leg kick or arm movement may also be used.

Suspension figures require practice, effort, and skill, but when properly executed, they are fascinating and fun to do. Suspension figures are especially useful in improving balance and control, and they can be a welcome change from the usual figure and stroke movements. Suspensions add variety in your compositions and increase the vocabulary of movement from which to choose when interpreting a theme and music.

Additional variety in suspension figures can be achieved by trying other methods of starting or finishing than those used in the variations in this chapter. Also, a suspension sequence can be changed by performing a Twist when in an inverted position and then continuing the sequence. All movements do not have to be performed slowly and smoothly. Some may be done quickly and forcefully, thus adding variety.

In addition to the common prone float positions and jellyfish float, the body can be suspended in many other positions. Some of these are shown in Figure 11.1. Naturally, the Inverted Vertical positions are the most difficult.

Contraction-Stretch (Figure 11.2): This is a good introduction to suspension figures because it includes contracting and stretching movements to change positions. Start in Back Layout, arms in V (A). Keeping arms in V, contract, drawing knees toward chin

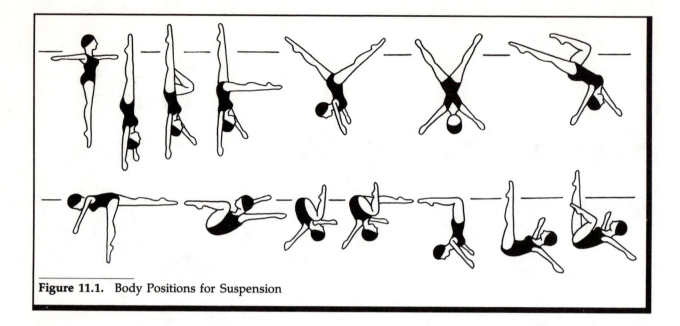

Figure 11.1. Body Positions for Suspension

so body is in tuck position (B). Using the momentum from the contraction, continue into partial Backward Tuck Somersault, arms in V (C). Open into Front Layout, arms still in V (D). Bring arms together overhead (E) and do half roll, finishing in Back Layout. Open arms to V and repeat but roll in opposite direction.

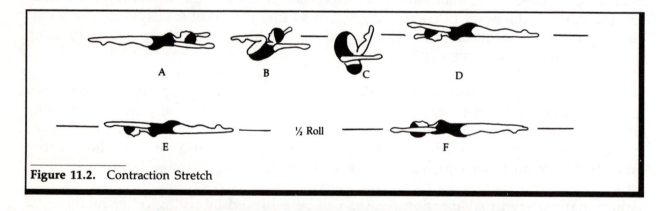

½ Roll

Figure 11.2. Contraction Stretch

Technique Tips

1. When changing from A to B, keep feet at surface.
2. When opening from Tuck to Front Layout, start when body is approximately in the position shown in C.

Sub Suspension (Figure 11.3):   Start in Back Layout, arms in V (A). Contract, tucking body at surface (B). Raise l. leg to vertical (C), which will cause body to sink. Balance in this position. Straighten r. leg so body is in Double Ballet Leg Sub (D). Pause. Bend l. leg (E). Bend r. leg to F. Face and legs, from knees to toes, will surface. Open to Back Layout, arms in V (G).

Figure 11.3. Sub Suspension

Technique Tips

1. When body is in Sub position, arms are in T position or slightly higher.
2. Water level in Sub positions will vary according to the Sub position used and your buoyancy.

Arabesque (Figure 11.4): From Back Layout, arms in V (A), raise r. leg, keeping it straight, and at the same time raise r. arm to meet it (B). Let body tip forward, bending l. knee and keeping r. hand to r. foot (C). Open the body and arch (D). The r. arm trails backward through the water at the surface, and the l. arm moves forward as body pendulums to E. Finish with r. arm backward and l. arm forward at surface.

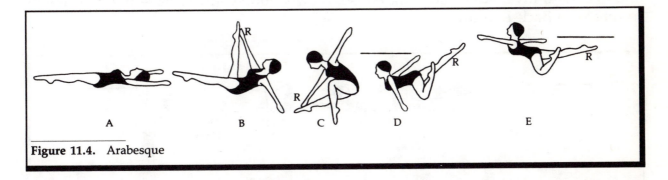

Figure 11.4. Arabesque

Tuck, Pike, Arched, Vertical—TPAV (Figure 11.5): From Back Layout, arms in V (A), contract (B) and do Somersault backward to Inverted Tuck (C). Straighten legs to inverted Pike (D). Do not pause but immediately arch body and raise one leg overhead to Scissors Split (E). Straighten body, raising back leg to vertical and bending forward leg so body is in Inverted Vertical Bent Knee position (F). Exchange position of legs (G). Finish by tucking and somersaulting backward or by arching and finishing as Foot-First Dolphin.

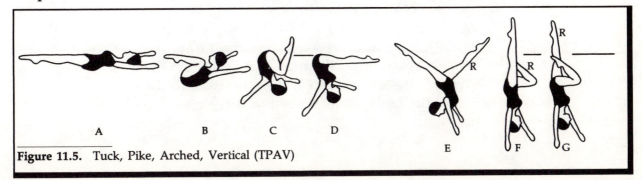

Figure 11.5. Tuck, Pike, Arched, Vertical (TPAV)

Spearfish-Scissors Combination (Figure 11.6):   From Back Layout, arms in V (A), contract, raising r. leg, bending l. knee, and raising arms forward (B). Tip backward to Inverted Spearfish position (C). Straighten body to Inverted Vertical, r. knee bent (D). Open legs to Scissors Split, arching body (E). Bend knee of forward leg (F) and let body pendulum feetfirst to Vertical (G).

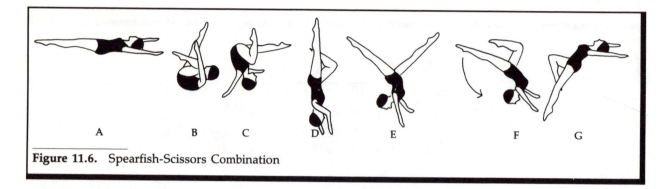

Figure 11.6.   Spearfish-Scissors Combination

Suspension Kip and Reverse (Figure 11.7):   From Back Layout, arms in V (A), contract, tucking body and keeping toes at the surface and arms in V (B). Tip backward into Inverted Tuck (C), arms approximately in T position. Slowly open the legs from knees, keeping head forward and back toward bottom (D). Completely straighten body slowly and evenly to Inverted Vertical (E). Pause. Slowly and evenly reverse the movements to return to Back Layout.

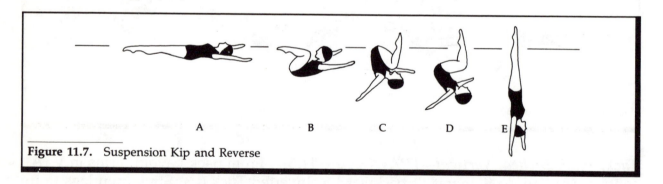

Figure 11.7.   Suspension Kip and Reverse

Technique Tips

1. Keep head forward when straightening to Inverted Vertical.
2. At the start of the straightening movement (D), the face is toward the knees.
3. When reversing the movements, begin by first bending the head forward, then rounding the back and bending at the hips and knees. On the reverse, the feet remain at the surface, and the rest of the body floats up to the surface to Tub position.

Potpourri Suspension Figures: Assume one of the inverted positions and move from it to two or more different positions. For example, move from Inverted Vertical to V Split, to Inverted Vertical, to Fishtail, to Bent Knee, to Scissors Split. Make up your own combinations using various methods to start and finish.

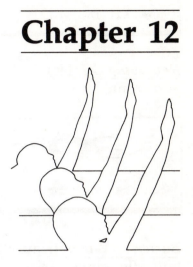

Chapter 12

Variations That Interpret

Ideas for aquatic variations can come from all around us—things, ideas, persons, events, places, objects, or animals can all suggest certain types of movements or qualities of movement. This chapter contains a few examples to help you develop your own variations based on what is important or interesting to you.

Puppet Ballet Leg (Figure 12.1):   From Boat (A), bend r. leg (B). Raise r. leg to position in C and to D. Extend to Vertical (E). Reverse the movements to return to Boat. Repeat, using l. leg, traveling throughout.

Figure 12.1. Puppet Ballet Leg

> **Technique Tips**
> 1. Imagine you are a puppet and have strings attached to your knees and toes.
> 2. Perform with precision and crispness.
> 3. Pause in each position.
> 4. Keep r. thigh vertical (B through E).

The Eel (Figure 12.2):   Do Dolphin Kick with body on the side and the arms extended overhead, at or below the surface.

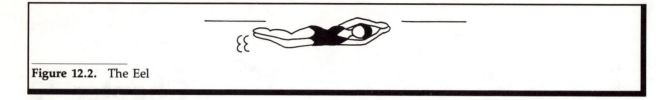

Figure 12.2.   The Eel

__Revolving Eel__ (Figure 12.3):   Do a series of Dolphin Kicks with the body on side, back, and front.

Figure 12.3.   Revolving Eel

__Butterfly Wings__ (Figure 12.4):   This variation interprets the opening and closing of butterfly wings. Assume Inverted Open Kneeling position (A). Twist in this position while smoothly and slowly opening legs to V (at surface), keeping knees and thighs together (B), and closing them (C). Repeat several times. Note that the opening of the legs to V involves the legs only from the knees to the toes.

Figure 12.4.   Butterfly Wings

__The Sprinkler__ (Figure 12.5):   From Boat (A), raise r. leg overhead, arching into Scissors Split (B). Make half Twist, closing legs during Twist (C) and opening into Scissors Split at the finish with other leg forward (D). Repeat, making half Twist in the same direction (E, F).

Technique Tip
1. Straighten the body when in Inverted Vertical (C, E) and arch when legs are in Scissors Split.

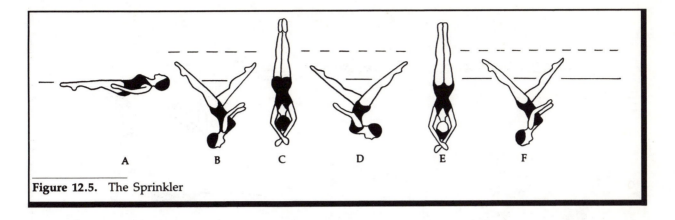

Figure 12.5.   The Sprinkler

The Rocket (Figure 12.6):   Start Dolphin (B). Tuck (C) and do partial Backward Somersault to Vertical (D). Scoop with arms to submerge feetfirst. Pike underwater (E) and scull toward surface in Double Ballet Leg Sub position. Just before head surfaces (F), thrust to Inverted Vertical Bent Knee position (G) and let body drop rapidly headfirst. Try for maximum height on thrust.

Figure 12.6.   The Rocket

Shooting Star (Figure 12.7):   Do Double Ballet Leg Sub to submerge (D). As soon as toes are below surface, tuck and perform Forward Tuck Somersault (E) to Inverted Tuck position (F). Perform Bent Knee Kip (G), thrusting as high as possible. Submerge headfirst (H), straightening bent knee. Arch body and rise to surface feetfirst (I), finishing as Foot-First Dolphin. This figure was originated by Henry Gundling, founder and first president of the International Academy of Aquatic Art (IAAA).

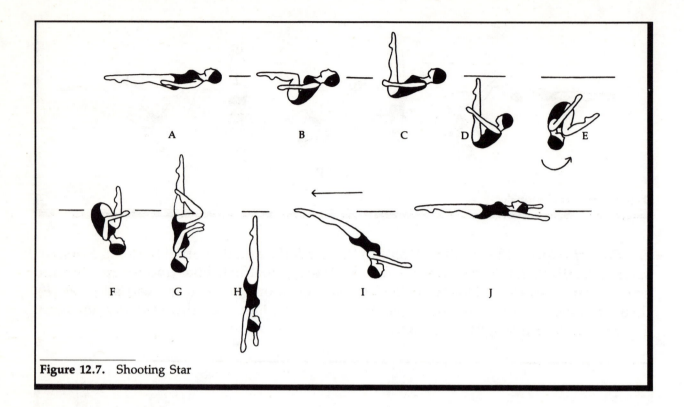

Figure 12.7. Shooting Star

Chapter 13

Using Objects in Variations

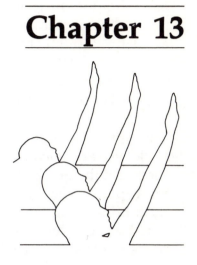

Using objects in the water can help you add to your interest and enjoyment, increase your skill in the water, extend your vocabulary of aquatic movement, discover new variations and types of aquatic movement, and originate compositions making use of these objects.

What objects can you use? Some of the more common ones include hoops, sticks, wands, canes, batons, poles, balls, hats, kickboards, swim fins, small parasols, scarves or streamers, inner tubes, artificial flowers, candles, and fans.

You need to take the object into the water and experiment with it to find out how best to use it. Here are some ways of doing this.

1. Find as many ways as you can to hold the object. Don't use only the fingers or the hand. Try other parts of the body, such as between the legs, between an arm and the side of the body, and so on. The grips used in floating-pattern work may be useful. In exploring the possibilities, you will be surprised at how many there are.

2. Develop stroke movements that you can do with the object.

3. Practice figures with the object to see which will be effective.

4. Think about all the movements you can do with the object that you can not do without it.

5. Get a partner or two and see what can be done with the object and more than one person.

The following reports contain a variety of unique ideas for using objects in compositions for performance. For example, Beulah Gundling (1971) has found that a parasol can be useful in performance.

During part of my composition, "Promenade," I use a small parasol in the water. Since I couldn't find the type of parasol I wanted, I made my own out of wire coat hangers and a curtain rod for a handle.

By experimenting in the water, I found that I could grasp the parasol in either hand or in both hands. I could hold it erect, or on a diagonal, or even upside down, by grasping it at the tip. I found I could move it forward and backward, from side to side, in a circle or partial circle. It could also be twirled.

The appearance of the movements could also be varied by the tempo, the force and the quality with which they were performed. Since the parasol didn't float, nor did I wish to discard it in the pool, I had to use surface-type movements such as leg kicks with the body vertical, on the side, and on the back. Marching and Waterwheel also worked well. Shark was possible, though I didn't use it. (p. 153)

At an International Aquatic Art Festival, the Peterborough (Canada) Ornamental Swim Club presented a duet entitled "Mexican Hat Dance," and the girls came out wearing huge Mexican hats. After the deckwork the girls entered the water, and the hats went with them. During part of the composition the hats floated on the surface while the girls performed around them, as in the land version of the Mexican hat dance. At other times the girls performed figures making use of the hats (see Figure 13.1), and, of course, at times the hats were also worn on their heads.

A number of interesting compositions have resulted from using hula hoops in the water. Solos, duets, trios, and group numbers have made effective use of these hoops. A group composition titled "Les Rondes Bleu" was performed by the Aquiana Swim Club, College of The Desert (California). It was coached by Frances Evans Sweeney and received Highest Honors in the IAAA International Festival. Four blue hula hoops were used in a number of ingenious ways in this composition for twelve girls.

A huge blue hoop, made in sections so that it could be taken apart, was used for a floating pattern composition, "Suspension," by Glenbrook (Illinois) North High School. The hoop floated, and the girls, costumed in the same shade of blue as the hoop, performed attractive patterns outside and inside the hoop.

Even castanets have been used in aquatic compositions. In the following report Beulah Gundling (1971) describes her experience.

Having learned to play castanets while studying Spanish dance a number of years ago, I decided to use them in a Spanish aquatic composition. At first I felt very much hampered and limited, since the castanets had to be held firmly in place when not being played, making sculling im-

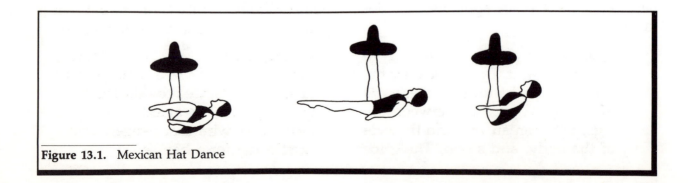

Figure 13.1. Mexican Hat Dance

possible and decidedly cutting down power on all other arm movements.

However, the more I experimented with movements in the water while holding the castanets, the more I discovered could be done, and for figure-type movements I found the suspension, stretching, contraction and rolling type ideal. The result was a successful composition and the discovery of figure movements which could be done without sculling. It is also possible to use finger cymbals in the water (as in my composition "Cymbalese"). (p. 157)

A very entertaining composition was a group number titled "Ball Aquatics" (see Figure 13.2) performed by Wright College (Chicago) at an IAAA Festival. Here is a report written by Bernice "Bee Cee" Hayes, coach, and Donna Glinka, one of the performers (cited in Gundling, 1971).

The idea for our composition originated after seeing a Danish rhythm number on TV. However, we immediately decided that we would not try to borrow or copy from the land movements, but, rather, to originate movements that were suitable to water skills. We tried to avoid comparison by giving our composition the title "Ball Aquatics" rather than "Rhythm Balls."

From the very start, this composition was fun. The fun began when we tried to control a slippery wet ball in the water. It was intriguing and challenging to do figures with a ball, and it was a good creative activity for a team.

None of the figures were executed with complete submergence because the ball kept above the water the part of the body that held it. We were able to do the following figures and strokes with the ball between the feet: Dolphin, Surface Dive, Kip, Pike Somersault, Oyster, Kip Twist, and variations of these. Later, some other figures added were: Swordfish and Heron done with ball in bent knee, Shark done with ball in bent knee instead of hand, and Bent Knee Eiffel Tower with the ball in bent knee.

You will find that many surface patterns can be developed with the ball held in the hands or with the feet. The activity is appealing to both swimmers and audience. (p. 157)

Figure 13.2. Ball Aquatics

Part III
Fun With Variations for More Than One Swimmer

Chapter 14

Stroke Variations for Two or More Swimmers

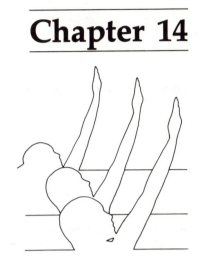

Strokes and stroke variations can be used by two or more performers to add excitement and movement to any composition or routine. In fact, entire compositions can be developed that contain only strokes and stroke variations. You will be amazed at what can be accomplished with perfect synchronization, pattern changes, stroke variations, hand expressions, and head focus. This chapter contains ideas for stroke variations to help you perform and practice stroking for synchronization and movement.

The Crossover

Do Back Crawl side by side, starting the pull with r. arm (Figure 14.1). After finishing a pull with the l. arm, swimmer *one* does Revolving Crawl, rolling onto the front across swimmer *two*, while *two* continues to do Back Crawl, pulling with the right. *One* continues Revolving Crawl, rolling onto the back, while *two* does Back Crawl, pulling with the left. *One* is now on the other side of *two*. This is accomplished by *two* moving ahead a bit and lowering the legs (continue the Flutter Kick) as *one* starts the Crossover. Then *two* slows down and *one* speeds up so that the two are side by side upon completion of the Crossover. The sequence may be repeated with *two* doing the Revolving Crawl and going across *one*. The body rolls to the right during Revolving Crawl on the Crossover.

Figure 14.1. The Crossover

Tandem Swimming

Tandem swimming is usually performed by two swimmers, though it is possible with more, using certain strokes and connections. In Chain Formation the feet of *one* are at either the neck, armpits, or waist of *two*. Illustrations of connections may be found in chapter 19, ''Floating Patterns.''

Tandem on Back (Figure 14.2): Use Elementary Backstroke, Inverted Breaststroke, Back Crawl, or variations of these strokes. Swimmer *one* uses only arms; *two* uses arms and legs.

Figure 14.2. Tandem Swimming on Back

Tandem on Front (Figure 14.3): Use Breaststroke, Crawl, or variations of these strokes. *One* uses only arms; *two* uses arms and legs.

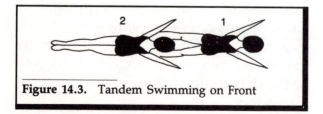

Figure 14.3. Tandem Swimming on Front

Mixed Tandem (Figure 14.4): *One* is on back; *two* on the front. *One* does Inverted Breaststroke with arms only; *two* does Breaststroke using arms and legs.

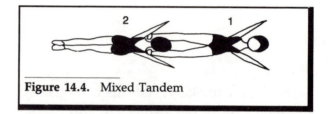

Figure 14.4. Mixed Tandem

Side by Side on Back (Figure 14.5): Inside arm is around back of partner, gripping waist with hand. Stroke, scull, or pull using outside arm only and do Flutter Kick with the legs.

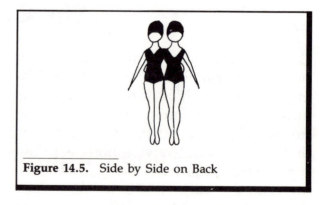

Figure 14.5. Side by Side on Back

Shadow and Mirror Swimming

Shadow and Mirror movements by two persons can add interest and variety to aquatic compositions and are also fun. Swimmers perform identical movements simultaneously with no body contact either side by side or with one person directly below the other.

In Shadow movements the swimmers face the same direction (Figures 14.6 through 14.8). In Mirror movements the swimmers face each other (Figures 14.9 and 14.10). Strokes such as Breaststroke, Inverted Breaststroke, and Sidestroke are usually used, but variations are also possible. Some figures and figure variations can also be shadowed or mirrored. As with all skills—and particularly when two or more persons are involved—you must experiment to find not only what movements can be used but also ways of getting into and out of a Shadow or Mirror sequence. After developing the variation and the transitions in and out, practice is essential to develop skill in synchronization and execution.

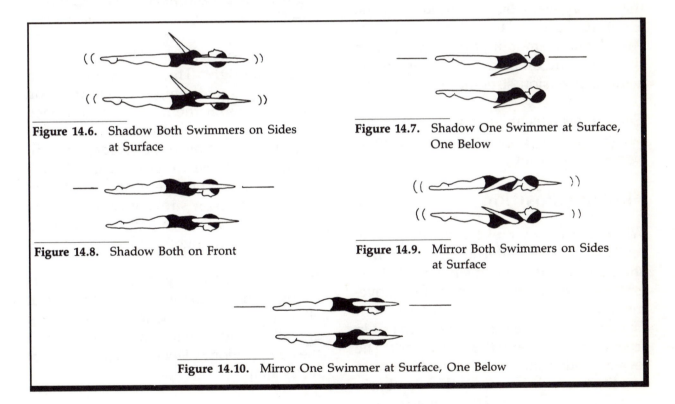

Figure 14.6.   Shadow Both Swimmers on Sides at Surface

Figure 14.7.   Shadow One Swimmer at Surface, One Below

Figure 14.8.   Shadow Both on Front

Figure 14.9.   Mirror Both Swimmers on Sides at Surface

Figure 14.10.   Mirror One Swimmer at Surface, One Below

Group Stroking and Formations

A great variety of surface designs are possible with four or more swimmers stroking in formation. Swimmers may be side by side, in single file, or in a stagger formation making patterns such as circle, square, triangle, or other designs (Figure 14.11). To watch a large group stroking and changing into endless number of patterns is really exciting. The water sounds, the patterns, the movement, and the precision make it one of the purest forms of synchronized swimming.

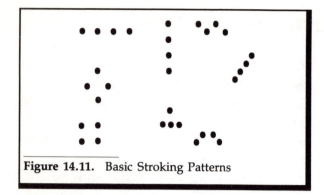

Figure 14.11. Basic Stroking Patterns

To be effective, precision and sameness of style are essential. Each swimmer must have exactly the same stroke, arm position, body position, and timing. Getting each swimmer to look the same is harder than it may seem, but it is the key to good group stroking and formation swimming. An adequate amount of practice, both in the water and on land, is the only way to achieve precision stroking.

Certain basic techniques will help to develop a group of swimmers into a precision stroking unit.

Starting Position

When practicing stroke drills or getting ready to start a pattern, each swimmer should be in the same position so that the group is synchronized from the first movement. One of the easiest positions to start from is to have the l. arm stretched out in front of the body and the r. arm back. The legs are either standing on the bottom in a split stance, l. leg forward, r. leg back, or providing support if the water is deep. The head should be still and forward, and the shoulders are just under the surface of the water. The arms should also be just below the surface. From this position the first stroke will always be with the r. arm. This position is adaptable to any stroke that will be performed, and it assures a proper start.

Guiding

Regardless of the style of stroke being used, the patterns must keep together in the proper position, with lines straight. No matter how quickly the pattern changes, each swimmer must know where to *guide* to keep things in the right place. *Guiding* is a term that refers to looking to a focus point or person without compromising the stroke being used. It will take practice to peek out of the corner of your eye at the person next to you or quickly to focus on the wall or ceiling to make sure you are in position. But if done correctly, the guiding process should never be noticed by a spectator.

Generally, swimmers will guide forward and to the right. This puts the responsibility for proper timing and placement on the swimmer at the far front right. Each person will guide to the swimmer either directly in front or to the r. side, or both, depending on the pattern. Figure 14.12 illustrates how to guide to the key swimmer for some basic stroking patterns. Keep in mind that with each pattern change the guiding will change.

Choreograph head positions and focus changes (more about this later) that will allow you to get a good look at your lines and allow you to make corrections within the composition. Clever choreography can really help.

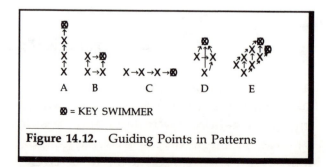

Figure 14.12. Guiding Points in Patterns

Counting

Counting every stroke is a must for large groups. Two common methods are used for counting in large-group stroking compositions, and you can choose the method you think will work best for your group.

Counting Upon Entry: The count for each stroke occurs as the hand *enters* the water. This method of counting has several advantages. First, it helps regulate the hand's entry into the water, which can get sloppy if not counted. Second, it is adaptable to all types of strokes. For example, strokes such as Bent Arm can be accommodated by counting the lift of the elbow as an *and*. From the starting position already described, using Bent Arm Stroke, the count would be *and* (for the lift of the elbow) *1* (for the entry of the r. arm) *and* (for the lift of the l. elbow) *2* (for the entry of the l. hand). Another advantage of this type of count is that it adapts to any timing or tempo changes, such as pauses or double time.

Counting on Recovery: Counting on recovery occurs when the arm lifts *out* of the water, for example, when the elbow bends up and out of the water for the Bent Arm Stroke. This type of counting also results in a definite style of stroking because the arm lift is more exaggerated than when counting with a different method. A large group can be taught similar stroke styles more quickly with this method, but it has several limitations. For example, this method of counting cannot be used very well with strokes other than those that have a definite or partial arm lift. It also does not adapt very well to timing changes or combining many stroke styles.

Regardless of the method you use or develop, however, stay with it and be consistent. Every stroking pattern and composition must be counted in the same manner, or you will never develop the type of precision pattern swimming that becomes automatic to trained swimmers.

In addition, remember to coordinate the kicks and other underwater movements with the counts of the arm strokes, especially the Sidestroke Kick. The kick must be performed on a definite count by everyone at the same time. Regular Flutter Kicks or the Eggbeater do not need to be counted, but make sure that each swimmer is doing the same type of kick or propulsion. The starting and ending of kicking sequences should, however, have a count.

Basic Arm Strokes

Bent Arm: From the stroking starting position, bend the r. elbow so that it is over the shoulder. The elbow will be pointed up, the upper arm fairly close to the head, and the thumb near the armpit. The head should remain still and focused forward, and the l. shoulder will drop slightly. Reach out with the r. arm to enter the water, fingertips first, about a foot in front of the body so that the arm is at a forty-five degree angle upon entry. After entry, any underwater pull can be used, but a shallow Bent Arm Pull will most quickly allow the elbow to get back into position for the next stroke. Repeat with l. arm. The body is on an angle in the water with the legs dropped for an underwater kick with no splash.

Straight Arm: From the stroking starting position, lift the r. arm out of the water just enough so that it is about an inch above the surface. With the palm facing the surface of the water, swing the arm forward to a position in front of the body and in line with the shoulder. The arm should be perfectly straight and just above the water surface on the swing forward. The whole arm enters the water in front of the shoulder at the same time and then executes a shallow Bent Arm Pull to behind the body to get into position for the next stroke. Repeat with l. arm. The head should be still, legs dropped for an underwater kick, and the shoulders even and just under the surface of the water.

High Arm: From the stroking starting position, lift the r. arm about an inch above the surface. Rotate the arm so that the palm is facing up. Lift the arm up and over the head to enter in front of the body and with the arm in line with the shoulder. Keep the arm as close to the head as possible on the lift-over. When first learning this stroke, it helps to have a specific count for the place in the stroke where the arm is next to the ear. This will help not only with the timing of the lift-over but also with keeping all arms close to the head and at the same angle. The whole arm enters the water at the same time and executes a shallow Bent Arm Pull back to the starting position. Repeat with l. arm. The legs are dropped for an underwater kick.

Swish Stroke: The Swish Stroke is a Straight Arm Stroke that is performed at the surface of the water instead of just above the surface. If held at a forty-five degree angle, the palm of the hand will create a strong splash as the arm swings around. If a smaller or more delicate splash is desired, angle only the fingertips to swish the water.

Sidestroke: Sidestrokes are usually used as transitions between stroke changes or for changing patterns, direction, or tempo. Several variations of the stroke can be used for different effects in a composition.

1. From any position in the water, extend an arm to the side of the body and lean toward it. (For a direction change, extend the arm toward the direction you wish to go and roll into the side position.) The other arm should be held in a position on top of the hip. Once in this side position, the arm being held on top of the hip lifts out of the water and over the head to meet the extended arm, where it enters the water. The arm then pulls back to a position on top of the hip. This Overarm Sidestroke can be used with an easy Flutter Kick on the side or with the traditional Scissors Kick. Keep in mind, however, that a Scissors Kick must be synchronized with other swimmers. If maximum propulsion is not needed, a Flutter Kick can stabilize the body and is not as distractive as a Scissors Kick.

2. A Sidestroke Roll stroke can be used to quickly and effectively change direction. From any position, get into the side position described in *Sidestroke.* Contract by bringing the arms and knees in toward the chest, staying on the side. Roll forward by dropping the top shoulder toward the surface of the water. As soon as the shoulder drops, the roll can be executed as far as desired to make the direction change needed. Extend the bottom arm overhead and parallel to the bottom of the pool, while the legs extend and kick into the side position. Keep the head out of the water during this stroke. The

Sidestroke Roll can be modified to eliminate the roll simply by bringing the legs under the body after contracting and leaning to the opposite direction before extending back into the Sidestroke position.

Turns and Pattern Changes

In addition to the turns and direction changes that can be done by modifying the basic strokes, there are other techniques that will help you develop effective stroking pattern changes.

Three-Point Turn (Figure 14.13): This turn can be used with any forward stroke, but it is best to learn it using the Straight Arm Stroke, beginning in the stroking starting position (l. arm out, r. arm back). From the stroking starting position, stroke right (count 1), stroke left (count 2), but keep the l. arm at the surface of the water in the entry position instead of pulling underwater. Stroke right (count 3), placing the arm on the surface of the water on a diagonal. At the same time the r. arm is moving to the diagonal, drop the l. arm to a position near the l. hip. The body at this point should still be leaning forward, with the head still and eyes focused straight ahead. Lift the l. arm (count 4) into a backstroke while rotating the upper body onto the back by pulling the r. arm (diagonal) to the body and giving a Scissors Kick with the legs if needed. The head will be pointed at a right angle to the previous forward direction. Keep the legs dropped down if you wish to move immediately into another forward stroking sequence.

The best count to use for this sequence is ''1, 2, Diagonal, Back'' for the four counts involved.

From the position on the back, with the legs dropped down, you can move into an unlimited number of positions. You can stay on the back for a Backstroke sequence; the l. arm can be brought up into a walk-out type of movement for a stationary pose; the r. arm can swish around and stop at any position. Once mastered, the Three-Point Turn will be a vital part of your stroking skills.

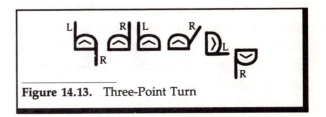

Figure 14.13. Three-Point Turn

Swish Turn: From any position or stroke, drop the legs underneath the body and extend an arm in front of the body at the surface of the water. Keep the other arm down near the hip. Angle the palm of the extended arm so that it will catch the desired amount of water. Use the arm that is under the water near the hip to press and scoop to turn the body rapidly. A Scissor Kick can also be added for more speed. As the body turns, the angled palm will splash in a swish, which can be stopped at any desired position. This type of Swish Turn is most effective when performed quickly and unexpectedly in a composition. It can also be added at the end of a stroke. Keep in mind that the more Vertical the body is, the faster you will be able to swish. Practice bringing your legs from a kicking position behind you, which would be used in stroking, to underneath you for a Vertical body position. This movement must be smooth and must fit in with the movements of the arms so that your swish will not appear jerky.

Cross Into (Figure 14.14):   The Cross Into is a way of merging, or passing, two lines of swimmers without breaking the stroking sequence. Line A and Line B both stroke in the same direction, about five feet apart. On a designated r. arm count, Line B quickly turns on the diagonal, toward Line A. Both lines continue stroking, with Line A stroking straight ahead and Line B stroking on a diagonal. Line B will enter Line A with each swimmer entering the line *behind* the swimmer that was next to him or her before the Cross Into. Designate a l. arm count to be the stroke that turns Line B to the same direction as Line A so that all swimmers are stroking in a single file line.

The key to a successful Cross Into is quick, sharp quarter turns to the diagonal and back to the original forward direction.

A Cross Into is most successful when it takes no more than four counts to perform: Count 1 is the first quarter turn to the diagonal, counts 2 and 3 are the strokes to get into Line A, and count 4 is the last quarter turn to get in single file formation with everyone facing the same direction.

Line A may have to slow down the speed, *but not the timing,* of their strokes to permit Line B to merge at the right place, or they may have to speed up. Only practice will determine the adjustments that need to be made.

The Cross Into can also be adapted to a Cross Thru by continuing the diagonal stroking of Line B until they have passed Line A.

Line A can Cross Into Line B by simply reversing the arms for the counts described above, with the first stroke being with the l. arm. The speed of either line can also be adjusted so that Line B could enter in front of Line A swimmers, if desired. What is important is that swimmers in both lines continue to stroke together on the same tempo throughout the merging of lines, and that the lines *stay straight.*

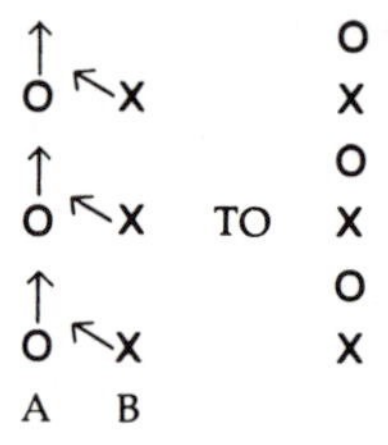

Figure 14.14.   Cross Into

Pivots (Figure 14.15):   Instead of using individual swimmers to change formations, Pivots use entire lines to create unusual and intriguing patterns.

A basic Pivot can rotate a line around a middle *anchor* swimmer or turn a line of swimmers by rotating around the end anchor.

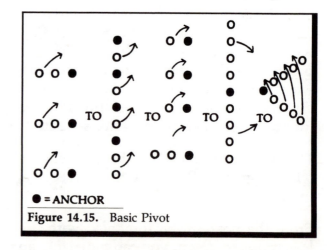

● = ANCHOR

Figure 14.15.   Basic Pivot

More elaborate Pivots can move a long line of swimmers around a center circumference like a wheel, or several short lines of swimmers can be transformed into a constantly changing, dynamic series of patterns similar to what you would see in drill team marching exhibitions.

Pivots are usually performed with lines of three or more swimmers. In a Basic Pivot, one end-person becomes the pivot around which the other swimmers will rotate. The pivot person continues to stroke on the same timing as the other swimmers, but he or she will stroke in place rather than move forward. The pivot person will, however, turn the body slightly with each stroke to keep at the same angle as the swimmers pivoting around. The swimmers who are not the pivot must adjust the strength of their underwater pulls so that their strokes can be synchronized on top of the water even though each swimmer is swimming a different distance in the same amount of strokes. The pivot person will not move forward at all, and the swimmer at the other end of the line will have to swim the greatest distance.

Lines must be kept straight to perform Pivots well. The line must move as a unit. Avoid letting the middle of the line sag back, creating a sloppy line and Pivot. Try to keep each swimmer's shoulders in line with the others and to keep the shoulders back and head high as much as possible. Keep chins up and focus high on Pivots for a better effect.

If Pivots are moving together to form a straight line or a pattern and then quickly breaking off into more Pivots for more patterns, choreograph one or two counts so that each swimmer knows when to "hit" the correct position. This will make the patterns more noticeable and achieve a crisper, cleaner performance.

Timing and Focus

Unique changes in timing and focus are the icing on the cake that can be added to stroking after the fundamental skills have been mastered and the basic choreography completed. They make the composition special and add to audience appeal.

To move faster or slower through the water, most of the time you cannot change the tempo of the stroke. Therefore, you have to adjust your underwater pull. If you need to move quickly to cover a long distance, you will have to pull underwater very strongly, even if your above-the-water movements are very delicate. If you are moving too quickly and need to slow down or even stop to stroke in place, do not pull underwater, but rather let your hand slice through the water with no resistance or pull.

Swimming in Place

Swimming in place is a skill that will help any stroking sequence. The same stroke tempo is used as if you were moving, but the legs are dropped under the body and you stroke in one spot. This skill can be used to allow lines to catch up with one another and merge or pass. It is used by the anchor or pivot person in a Pivot, and it can be used just to slow a pattern down and control use of the pool.

Pauses

A pause can be a very dramatic tool for use in stroking sequences. An arm is held, usually at the point of entry into the water, for an extra count. A basic pause sequence would be stroke right (1), stroke left (2), half-stroke right to straight arm stretched in front of the body out from the shoulder (3), hold position (4), half-stroke left to straight arm stretched in front of the body (5), hold position (6), stroke right (7), stroke left (8).

Double Time

Double time is fun to do but requires a stroke that can be executed with a very shallow underwater pull so that the arms can get into the position for the next stroke quickly. Regardless of counting method or tempo, double time speeds the movement of the strokes so that twice as many strokes are executed in the same amount of counts. For example: right (1), left (2), right-left (3), right-left (4).

Head Focus

Choreograph definite head movements to go with the strokes, mood, and timing of your stroking sequences. Use a head movement to fill those little gaps or neat places in the music where you would love to add something. In addition to adding variety, a turned head will allow you to see where you are and to clean up any messy lines or off positions quickly, before they become noticeable. Combined with hand gestures and arm positions, head focus can be a primary source of expression for your creativity.

Some head movements you can use are turn to the side, look down, look up, roll, bend side to side, swim with the face in the water, and shrug the shoulders.

Stroking Practice

Of all the aquatic skills, stroking is probably the most adaptable to different, effective forms of practice. Whereas there is no substitute for stroking drills and pattern practice, much can be done in shallow water and even on land.

Land walk-throughs are an integral part of any performer's practice time, but they are especially useful with stroking sequences because you can closely approximate the actual skill on land that you will be doing in the water. Changes can be made quickly and easily, and the water time can be more efficiently used.

When land drilling, remember to count everything and to perform your strokes just as you would in the water. Don't get sloppy and just go through the motions. Perform actual strokes and get used to proper arm positions.

Walk-throughs in shallow water are also important. You can stand on the bottom, which helps you make quick changes but also allows you to get a feel for how much pull you will need with each stroke to make the necessary patterns.

When it's all put together, *swim, swim, swim,* and enjoy!

Chapter 15

Choreographing Precision Stroking Compositions

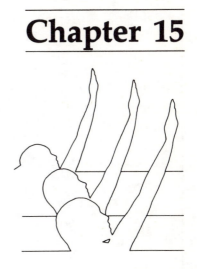

A stroking composition can be defined as a team number made up almost entirely of strokes. Its positive effect is achieved through precision. Strong swimmers are needed for a good stroking composition, and the strokes they acquire through practice must be efficient and stylistically similar.

When choreographing a stroking composition, you create variations in the *formation*, the *stroke patterns*, and the *strokes* themselves. A good combination of these variations will develop into an interesting composition. The skill of the swimmers and the choreographer will determine the degree of development possible.

To begin the choreography, first work out the formations. For example, a twelve-swimmer composition might start out in three lines with four abreast or in pairs or in single file. It could then change to another formation after about eight strokes, then change again. For an example, see Figure 15.1.

To avoid a disorganized look, have only a small number of swimmers change position at one time; thus a definite formation is held during the change. If everyone changes at the same time, there will be a few seconds when there is *no* formation. The principle is that even the movement of change must have an orderly look and must be visually clear and attractive.

After working out the formation, work out the stroke patterns. The music and formations will be your guides for this process. For example, four bent and four straight equal eight strokes; one bent, three straight, two bent, and two straight equal eight strokes; three front-turn, one back-turn (see Three-Point Turn, chapter 14) plus another three front-turn, one back-turn equal eight counts.

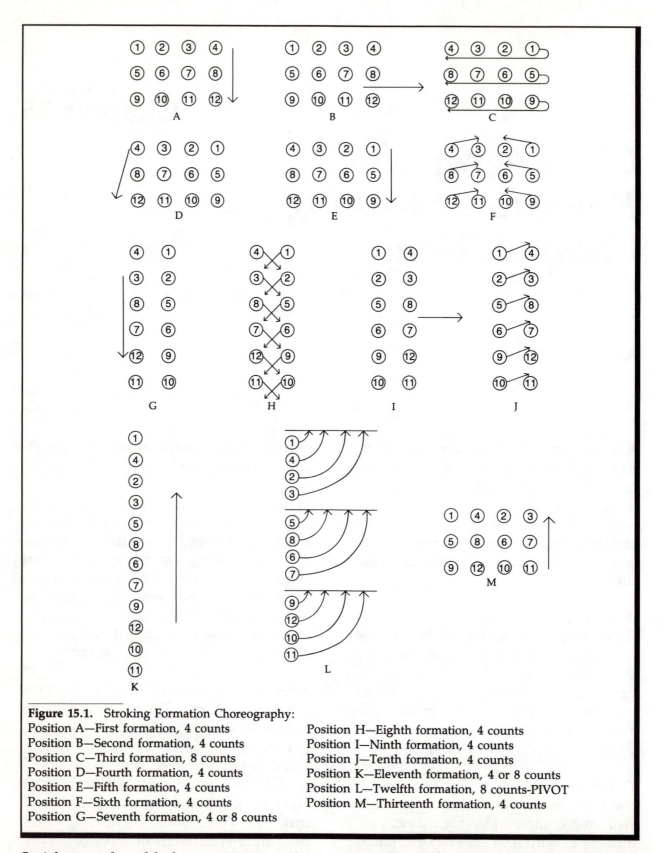

Figure 15.1. Stroking Formation Choreography:
Position A—First formation, 4 counts
Position B—Second formation, 4 counts
Position C—Third formation, 8 counts
Position D—Fourth formation, 4 counts
Position E—Fifth formation, 4 counts
Position F—Sixth formation, 4 counts
Position G—Seventh formation, 4 or 8 counts

Position H—Eighth formation, 4 counts
Position I—Ninth formation, 4 counts
Position J—Tenth formation, 4 counts
Position K—Eleventh formation, 4 or 8 counts
Position L—Twelfth formation, 8 counts-PIVOT
Position M—Thirteenth formation, 4 counts

Swishes can be added as an accent on the change of direction or on the change of formation. Changes of direction are also good places to put in variations, accents, and other frills. These additions give contrast emphasis. Also, try a Pivot in the water. It is fun but difficult to do correctly.

Instead of stroking to every beat, the swimmers can use their legs to keep the beat. For example, kick, kick, back, back plus kick, kick, back, back equal eight beats. This type of movement may be used when the music is so fast that it is impossible to take four strokes. The combination of kicks and strokes also gives a jazz effect and an uneven rhythm effect.

Varying the rhythm at different points creates more interesting choreography. For instance, in a four-beat sequence, the possibilities are (a) stroke to each beat, (b) take two beats for each stroke, thus taking only two strokes to four beats, or (c) kick, kick, stroke, stroke.

The variety of strokes will be determined by the mood and energy of the music. For instance, jazz will necessitate interpreting and using some jazz-like strokes. A very serious, slow composition will need slow, steady strokes to carry out the theme. In a stroking composition called ''Saints Go Marching In'' performed by the University of Illinois Chicago Aquianas, the team did an interpretive up-down movement with the r. arm, then two quick Bent Arm crawl strokes; it was up, down, stroke, stroke, up, down, stroke, stroke. The head followed the up-down movement, and the fingers were spread on the up but made a fist on the down. This is just one example of many variations that were used in this composition.

When choreographing, compose in sequences of reasonable length. The music will determine how many formations can be handled at a time. Choreographing the whole composition at one time should be avoided, but working with too short sequences is frustrating and may lack clear organization. Develop a sequence (unit) and work with it on deck before working it out in the water. If it is feasible in the water, then go on to another sequence. A unit will often look great on deck, but it becomes impossible in the water. Build one formation on another.

Strokes are fundamentally for the purpose of *moving* a swimmer in the water. Stroking numbers will very rarely use strokes while holding in place, but one of the great plus factors in stroking compositions is that the team is compelled to move real distances. Good choreographers take advantage of this. The swimmers should move from one end of the pool to the other and back again—they should not get stuck in one area. Increasing the distance moved increases the effect of the synchronization on the viewers.

Selecting interesting music is the key to a good composition because music provides the fundamental inspiration. You should be interpreting the music, not making formations and then finding music to sound good with the swimming. The music, and what it says, is the basis of the needed discipline—it determines the direction, dynamics, and style of the composition. If you start with dull, mediocre music, the composition is also likely to be dull and mediocre. Don't be afraid of dramatic or challenging music; it is better to start big and try to come up to the level of the music.

The costume should emphasize the head and arms because those elements show most prominently in the water. They should be bright and colorful but not heavy looking.

It is very difficult to work with twelve or sixteen swimmers because (a) each swimmer must be synchronized in time with the music, (b) each swimmer's movements must be synchronized with every other swimmer's movements, and (c) each swimmer must be synchronized in space in the pool with even lines and regular spacing.

A good soloist works to weld the strokes and figures with the beat of the music. With a team of twelve or sixteen, however, the coach must work to bring the angle of the arm and hand, the turn of the head, the curve of turn, the height of arm out of water, the direction of head, body, and legs of each of the swimmers into exact synchronization. The relative position in the water of each swimmer must also be synchronized exactly. But then, precision is what stroking compositions are all about.

When you see twelve or sixteen swimmers stroke down the pool looking as one, exactly on the beat of the music, with the sound of the strokes in the water exactly corresponding to the music, it is thrilling, and the extra effort needed to accomplish this challenge becomes clearly worth it. Try it—you'll like it!

This chapter was contributed by Frances Evans Sweeney of the University of Illinois, Chicago. It will help you put together and choreograph large-group stroking compositions. Under the direction of Fran Sweeney, the University of Illinois Chicago Aquianas and their alumni team at North Suburban YMCA in Northbrook, Illinois, have become known for their dynamic stroking routines.

Chapter 16

Sculling and Figure Variations for Two or More Swimmers

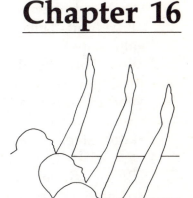

Figures and sculling that require more than one person also require special techniques. This chapter describes multi-person variations that are basic examples.

However, the possibilities for new creations with varying numbers of people are endless.

Sculling Variations

Sculling with two or more persons not only increases proficiency in sculling but also can be more enjoyable than practicing sculling alone. Refer to chapter 17 for additional descriptions and techniques for connections.

Chain Sculling: Connect feet to neck, scull with the arms at the sides of the body. When on the back, use Standard Scull to travel headfirst and Reverse Scull to travel feetfirst. Chain Sculling can be performed in the following positions:

1. Boat Chain: on backs, in Layout position.
2. Tub Chain: All swimmers assume a Tub position at the same time.

3. Tub/Boat: Alternate Tub and Boat positions by having the whole line scull in Boat position, change to Tub position, and back to Boat, or every other swimmer in the line changes into the Tub position, resulting in a staggered variation.
4. Canoe Chain: All swimmers perform Canoe using Standard Scull to move headfirst.

Tandem Sculling: Tandem sculling is usually performed with two swimmers, although these variations are possible with more.

1. Barge: Each swimmer is in Boat position (Back Layout) and is con-

nected at the ankles or higher. One swimmer performs Standard Scull, the other Reverse Scull.

2. Tub Barge: The same as Barge but each swimmer is in a Tub position. Boat and Tub positions may be alternated.

3. Boat/Tub: In this variation one swimmer is in the Boat position and the other in the Tub position. Boat and Tub positions may be alternated.

4. Propeller/Boat: Each swimmer is in Boat position, connected at ankles or higher. One swimmer performs Standard Scull, arms at the sides, while the other performs Propeller (Torpedo) Scull, arms overhead.

5. Propeller/Canoe: Swimmers are connected feet to feet; one is in Boat position, the other in Canoe. The swimmer in Boat position performs Propeller (Torpedo) Scull, arms overhead, while the other swimmer performs Canoe.

6. Boat/Canoe: Same as Propeller/Canoe but the swimmer in the Boat position performs Reverse Scull with arms at the sides.

Figure Variations

Planking, Two or More Persons (Figure 16.1):   Basic Planking is usually done with two persons, although it is possible with more. Begin in Back Layout, single file formation. Swimmer *two* grasps ankles or feet of swimmer *one*, grasping from underneath with the palms facing up. *Two* pulls *one* feetfirst at the surface while submerging just below *one*. At finish of pull, *two* releases grip and continues to glide headfirst in Boat position underneath *one*, surfacing just behind *one*. As *two* surfaces, legs should slide through *one*'s arms, which are extended so *one* can grasp ankles or feet of *two* and repeat the movement with *one* submerging.

Variations:

1. Plank and finish in Vertical position by tucking.

2. Split Plank: Spread arms and legs apart in V Split prior to Plank. Bring arms and legs together on Plank.

3. Dolphin Plank: Do not connect at finish but arch and perform a Dolphin. This may be done by one or all swimmers.

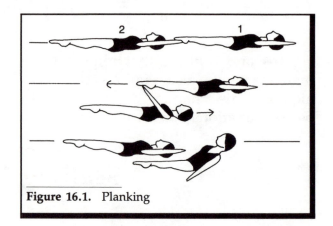

Figure 16.1.   Planking

Stacking, Three or More Persons (Figure 16.2):   Stacking is a type of Plank, but rather than gliding completely underneath the top person, each person stops his or her movement directly under the person above so that all are stacked one on top of the other. It is very effective in a composition because the movement is usually unexpected and is very dynamic if performed well with a number of people.

Begin as in Basic Plank, with each person grasping the ankles or feet of the person in single file at his or her head. All pull quickly and forcefully at the same time and

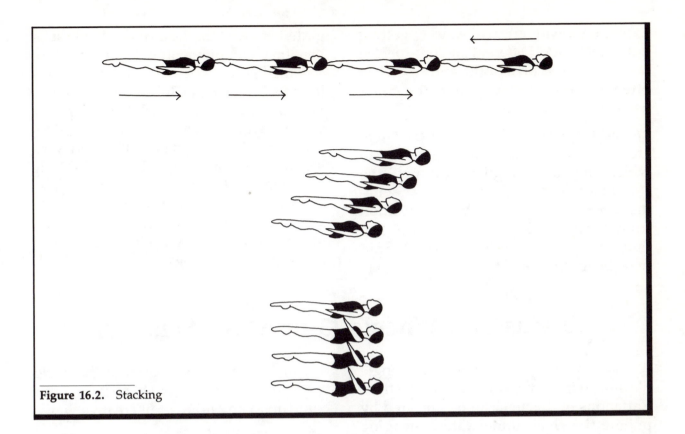

Figure 16.2. Stacking

submerge and glide under the person whom they pulled. The person at the beginning of the line is pulled across the surface of the water and remains on the surface. All others must submerge at different levels to get under the person above them. As each person gets directly underneath the person above, he or she grabs the waist of the person above and holds to keep the Stack together and even.

Technique Tips

1. The swimmers toward the end of the line may need to take a second pull to get under and in position. While doing any extra pulls, the arms should be bent and over the chest so that the elbows and arms cannot be seen outside the line of the body.
2. Be sure to pull and glide underneath before grabbing the waist of the person above you, or the Stack will be pulled out of line before anyone is in position.
3. An alternate way of pulling is to make the initial Chain connection by sliding the arms underneath the legs of the person whose feet are at the neck and grabbing above the knees rather than at the ankles.

Experiment with creative ways of getting out of the Stack. Different and unexpected fan-out moves, break-offs, and so on can often be more exciting than the Stack itself.

Thread the Needle, Two Persons: There are many variations of this movement in which one person glides through the V Split legs of the second person. Swimmer *one* may assume the V Split position from Porpoise, Kip, Double Ballet Leg Sub, or any other figure in which a V Split may be performed. Swimmer *two* may glide between the legs of *one* feetfirst or headfirst with momentum from sculling or sculling figures, a stroke, or a figure finishing as a Foot-First Dolphin, Swordfish, or Walkover. *One* may finish the V Split in various ways, such as bringing legs together and submerging headfirst; bringing legs together, arching body, and finishing as a Foot-First Dolphin; or bringing legs together, tucking, and somersaulting to surface. The figure may be repeated with *two* performing the V Split and *one* going through the split legs.

Chains and Wheels (3 or More Persons)

A Chain is formed by connecting a single file line with a feet-to-neck connection. Variations of this line can be executed by pulling the chain underwater, changing body positions, arm positions, and so forth. A Wheel is a Chain that pulls around to connect with the end person to create an unbroken circle.

Shark Chain: Form a Chain, feet to neck, on backs. Turn on sides. Arch bodies and do Shark. Top arm of each swimmer is extended overhead. The top arm of the second person in the Chain is extended along the side of the top leg of the lead swimmer.

Shark Wheel: Form a Shark Chain with four or more persons, with the lead person connecting with the end person to form a continuous connection.

Dolphin Chain (Figure 16.3): Swimmers in single file formation and connected feet to neck perform a Dolphin. The more persons there are, the deeper the lead swimmer will have to pull the chain before beginning the bottom curve of the Dolphin circle. As in a Dolphin performed by one person, an even circle should be executed, with all persons evenly arched. The Chain can turn over at the bottom of the circle to execute a Figure-Eight Dolphin, or it can come up in any number of creative ways.

Double Chain Dolphin: (Figure 16.4, position A): With a large number of swimmers the lead swimmer of the Chain can pull a circle smaller than is usually needed for the number of swimmers and finish the Dolphin circle before the end swimmers have been pulled down. The lead swimmer surfaces next to a swimmer still on the surface to form a double chain by hooking on to that person with a connection around the waist. As other swimmers surface, they also hook up side by side, and the circle continues rotating until all have hooked up in partners and one or more additional revolutions are made.

Foot-First Dolphin Chain: Same as Dolphin Chain except do a Foot-First Dolphin.

Mixed Dolphin Chain, Two Persons: Form Chain in Back Layout position, attaching at ankles. Swimmer *one* performs Dolphin pulling *two* down feetfirst so that *two* performs a Foot-First Dolphin while assisting with propulsion.

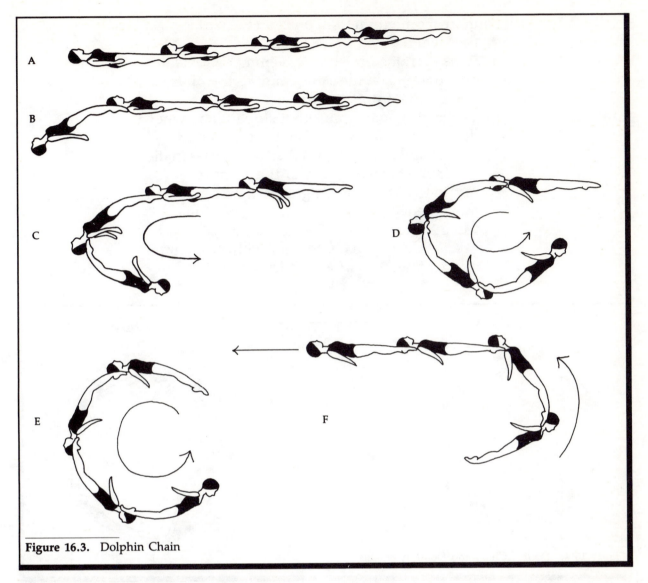

Figure 16.3. Dolphin Chain

Dolphin Wheel, Three or More Persons
(Figure 16.4, position B): First form a
Chain and do Dolphin Chain until Swimmer *one* nears the surface and can grasp
the last person's feet and attach them
around the neck so that a circle is formed.

Continue to do Dolphin Wheel one or
more revolutions.

Foot-First Dolphin Wheel: Similar to
Dolphin Wheel but do Foot-First Dolphin.

Technique Tips for Chains and Wheels

1. All pulls or other arm movements must be
   synchronized.
2. Practice each pull by counting out loud; use a
   count for each position the arms must move
   through to get ready for the pull in addition to
   the counts for the pull itself.
3. The more persons in the Chain, the more difficult the Chain will be to pull and control. Also,

more momentum from pulls on the surface will be needed.

4. Pulls do not stop when a swimmer submerges but continue on the same count as the pulls being executed on the surface.

5. The lead swimmer must not stop pulling when he or she surfaces but should continue to pull powerfully, on count, until all swimmers in the Chain have been pulled to the surface.

6. Try to avoid any extra grasping and grabbing movements when making connections for Chains and Wheels. The connections must be precise, and appear effortless with a minimum of movement of arms and legs.

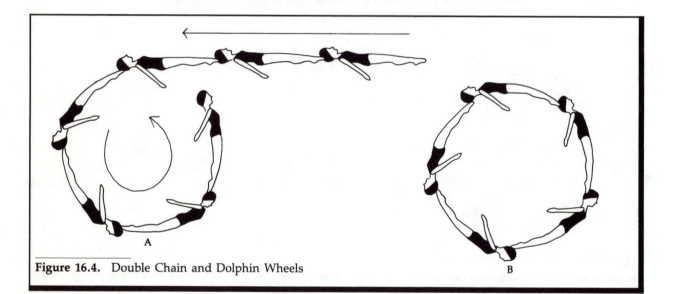

Figure 16.4. Double Chain and Dolphin Wheels

Chapter 17

Contact Variations

Contact figures aren't easy—execution and timing must be top rate for them to be successful. This means much practice with the same partner plus experimentation to find what will and will not work to achieve the best technique.

To be successful in some contact figures, one person should be shorter than the other. Also, both must have a good foundation in basic skills and be at the same relative level of skill.

As with regular figures, some contact figures are easier than others, and these should be learned first. Gradually add work on new figures as you perfect the basic ones.

Contact is made by one person holding onto the other in some figures, which means only one person has hands free for propulsive movements. In other figures the contact can be maintained without holding, so both persons can support or move the figure.

Sometimes only the start or part of a figure is done in contact. At other times the entire figure is done in contact.

In body contact work, the back of one person is usually on top of the front of the other person, with both facing in the same direction. However, it is possible to do some movements with the persons facing in opposite directions, especially while inverted.

Getting into and out of position skillfully is necessary for the contact figure to be successful, and you must experiment to discover ways of doing this and then practice to perfect them. It is also necessary to experiment to find where and how to hold on to the other person because this will vary according to each individual and each skill.

One way of getting into position for body contact work is to Plank to the point where one person is below the other. Clasp so that bodies are in contact and go directly into a contact figure.

A simple contact movement exercise is to bob in deep water, keeping contact, with only one person using the arms to rise and sink.

Some figures and movements that can be done in contact are Tub, Rolling, Somersault, Sailboat, Ballet Leg, Submarine, Dolphin, Walkover, Barracuda, and Kip. All thrusting figures are especially difficult to perform in contact but are very dynamic. Inverted Split movements and positions also yield many possibilities for

contact work. In Split positions, the legs can contact and change positions. Combined with some contact of the upper bodies and some changing body positions, unique combinations of contact leg work are unlimited.

Contact Dolphin (Figure 17.1):   Swimmer *one* places head on chest of *two*, who is underneath. *One* grasps back of thighs of *two*. *Two* furnishes propulsion throughout.

Figure 17.1.   Contact Dolphin

Contact Kip (Figure 17.2): *One* places head on chest of *two*. (The exact position will vary according to the individuals involved). *One* grasps around *two* as both draw the knees in to a Tub position. Both swimmers must be placed in such a way that the hips and knees can bend to get into position while maintaining contact. *Two* does Somersault into an Inverted

Tuck position and maintains support while the legs are lifted to Inverted Vertical. Remain in contact until all feet are below the surface. Experiment with different ways to hold, different positions on the body, and ways to support the figure. Practice until you find what works best for you and your partner.

Figure 17.2.   Contact Kip

Partial Contacts: These may be contact with the legs, feet, or another part of the body by two swimmers. In partial contacts both swimmers should be the same height. Strength and skill in sculling are also essential. Two examples to get you started experimenting on your own are the Spearfish Variation and Sub Spearfish Variation.

Spearfish Variation (Figure 17.3): In single file formation, feet to feet with body in Boat position, assume surface Tuck position, keeping toes touching. Raise one leg to Vertical to Spearfish (Flamingo) position, then angle the leg so feet touch or legs can cross at ankles. Contact is also maintained wth feet of bent legs. Use Reverse Hybrid Scull to hold position.

Figure 17.3. Spearfish Variation

Sub Spearfish Variation (Figure 17.4): In single file formation, feet to feet, do Double Ballet Leg Sub to submerge (no contact). Bend one leg so toes touch part-

ner's toes and overextend the other leg. Rise, keeping toes in contact, and bring straight legs forward so that toes touch.

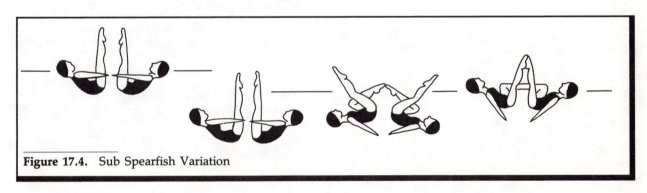

Figure 17.4. Sub Spearfish Variation

Chapter 18

Lifts and Thrusts

The information in the Shallow Water Lifts section of this chapter is from material by the late Bernice "Bee Cee" Hayes (1977). Bee Cee was a pioneer in developing shallow water coed lifts while she was coach-advisor at Wright College in Chicago. These lifts are usually done by couples, although some lifts may be done by more than two persons and of either sex or both sexes. Lifts are fun. Both men and women enjoy doing them. This material was originally written for mixed sex couples, so the "boy" is the person lifting and the "girl" is the person being lifted.

General Technique Tips for Shallow Water Lifts

1. Always practice away from the sides of the pool and other swimmers. Falls are commonplace but will never harm the girl if she tucks to break the impact and is far enough away to avoid hitting someone or something.
2. The practice and/or costume suit of the girl should help the boy's grip and not add to his problems. Avoid suits with lining. When a girl helps support herself as in a shoulder stand, it helps to have the boy wear something that covers the shoulders such as a tight shirt or leotard. Neither should use any cream or lotion on any part of the body.
3. All lifts are easier if the girl holds her breath at the start and during the lift.
4. When the girl starts from a standing position, she can help with a properly timed push from one or both feet.
5. Because the boy is standing in water, most lifts should be high enough to get the girl's head, hands, and feet out of the water.
6. Some basic lifts are easy to perfect. Others take time to develop strength and balance. Do not be discouraged if you are not successful for many weeks.
7. Approaches, as well as let downs,

or exits, are an important part of lifts. Work hard to make these smooth.

Approaches for Shallow Water Lifts

1. A stroke with turnover to layout, front or back.
2. Somersault (tuck or pike, front or back) into layout, standing, or lift position.
3. Walkover into layout, standing, or lift position.
4. Shark into desired position.

Let Downs or Exits for Shallow Water Lifts

Let downs or exits can be the most difficult part of the lift. In the simplest one, the boy drops under water until the girl touches the surface. The girl must then break any arch so that she can float noiselessly into a stroke or figure. In other exits, the girl somersaults, tuck or pike, from full or partial height into the water. The girl can even be thrown feetfirst into the water.

Basic Shallow Water Lifts

There are no absolute rules for any lift. Different body lengths, weights, and builds produce different centers of gravity and require different holds. If the end result is good, that is all that matters.

Following are some examples of a few of the different types of aquatic lifts. Many more are possible! Study the lifts used by figure skaters, gymnasts, cheerleaders, and dancers. These will give you ideas and some may also be adapted to aquatic lifts. Experiment!

Basic Dolphin Lift (Figure 18.1, position B):   Girl in arched position, back to boy, supported by boy's fully extended arms. Girl may be facing in either direction, but the lift is easier if girl's head is toward boy's back, feet forward. The girl's arms are extended parallel above the head, gracefully curved to continue the arc.

Approach: The easiest is for the girl to be in Back Layout, boy underwater below girl. Both hands of boy are on small of girl's back. Girl's weight is on the heel of the boy's hands. When learning, the boy should have both arms straight, elbows locked, standing in fairly deep water, before he attempts to lift her. However, the lift will look better if the boy is in shallower water, has bent arms when he starts to lift, then straightens his arms. Boy's stance is one foot forward, knee bent, back leg straight. Lift can also be from a stand, girl's back to boy.

Exit: Boy bends knees and goes underwater. Girl straightens from arch to layout as she touches surface of water. Another exit is for the boy to bend his arms and with controlled movements lower the girl to his shoulder.

Technique Tips

1. This is an easy, pretty lift but is often performed poorly. The boy must have both arms even.
2. The girl's body should be tense, not like a rag doll.

3. The girl's fingertips and toes should be out of the water, with body balanced so that the feet and hands are about equal distance from the water.

Dolphin Lift Variation (Figure 18.1, position A):   Basic Dolphin Lift, but boy supports girl with one hand centered on her back, fingers toward the head, with the other hand on side of leg, thumb on inside of leg, fingers spread on outside.

Bent Knee Dolphin Lift (Figure 18.1, position C):   Basic Dolphin Lift, but girl bends one knee. Foot of bent leg is at side of straight leg.

Bent Knee Dolphin Lift Variation: Girl's r. knee bent, boy has hand centered on girl's back, weight on ball of hand, the l. hand on the ankle of the girl's straight leg. Boy tips body of girl until it feels well balanced. Then the ankle is released, and the girl's body is held balanced on the hand on the back only, for a one arm lift. The boy's free arm is extended to the audience side and held above the water. During the approach, the boy's hands assume the hold underwater. The girl may assist lift by a slight push with the straight leg.

Figure 18.1. Dolphin Lifts

Basic Swan Lift (Figure 18.2):   Girl in arched position, front of her body toward water, supported by boy's straight arms, his hands at her waistline or high or low on her hips. Each boy finds his own balance point with this partner, and each elevation and arch position of the girl is a little different. Both arms lifted back is the prettiest position for the girl's arms, but this may be varied, such as bringing the arms forward with the arm on the audience side high or arms crossed in front.

Bent Knee Swan Lift: Basic Swan Lift with one knee bent. Foot of leg with bent knee is at the side of the straight leg. In a beautiful sequence the girl starts with Bent Knee Swan Lift, then straightens that leg into a Basic Swan Lift.

Figure 18.2. Swan Lift

Basic Handstand Lift: Shoulder stand with the girl facing boy and her hands on his shoulders. The boy has his hands on the girl's hips. With a little spring the girl is lifted over the boy's head. His arms are straight up, hers should be straight and stiff, angled back from the boy's shoulders. Her body is arched, head and legs held high.

Variation of Handstand Lift: Girl holds on to boy's arms. This is good for short girls. The lift will probably be higher.

Reverse Handstand Lift: From Back Layout with head toward boy, girl does Back Tuck Somersault, grasps boy's body or arms by reaching over her head. Boy grasps girl high on hip bones as she turns and lifts her by straightening his arms. The straighter the boy's hands are on the hip bones (fingers toward the girl's head), the straighter the lift will be.

Basic Arabesque Lift (Figure 18.4): Swimmers facing each other, boy's hands are at waist of girl. Lift girl straight up. One of girl's legs is held straight down along boy's body. The other is raised backward in an Arabesque position.

Basic Standing Lift (Figure 18.5): Boy stands with both legs bent. Girl stands on boy's thighs with both of her feet. The girl

Figure 18.3. Handstand Lift

Figure 18.4. Arabesque Lift

Figure 18.5. Standing Lift

has her back to the boy. The boy supports her with hands held on her legs (A). With three persons, the girl can be lifted to a standing position on the boy's chest (B).

Basic Kneeling Lift (Figure 18.6):   Girl on boy's shoulder, girl facing in either direction, one leg kneeling on shoulder of boy, the other raised back. Boy and girl clasp hands, and arms are extended to the sides, hers angled down, his angled up. It is important to keep arms straight and even.

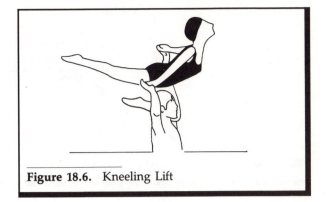

Figure 18.6.   Kneeling Lift

Thrusts and Deep Water Lifts

In thrusts, swimmer *one* thrusts swimmer *two* out of the water either headfirst or feetfirst. Thrusts are usually done in water deeper than the height of the persons involved.

Thrusting Flying Dolphin (Figure 18.7): *One* and *two* submerge facing each other. *One* stands on bottom in stride position, legs bent and hands clasped in front. *Two* puts one foot in clasped hands and own hands on *one's* shoulders for balance. *One* thrusts *two* as far out of the water as possible headfirst. *Two* arches in the air as in Dolphin, entering the water headfirst. Instead of clasping hands, *one* may place hands on *two's* hips for thrust.

Figure 18.7.   Thrusting Flying Dolphin

Thrusting Flying Porpoise (Figure 18.8): Started as Thrusting Flying Dolphin, but both persons face the same direction. *One* may thrust *two* up by grasping *two* at the hips. *Two* should help by bending knees and springing up as *one* thrusts. In the air, *two* pikes and enters the water headfirst as in Flying Porpoise done singly in shallow water.

Thrusting Inverted Vertical Figures-Deep Water Lifts: *One* submerges and assumes a position below *two*, while *two* may assume Inverted Tuck, Inverted Pike, Inverted Spearfish, and so forth, at surface. *One* puts hands, arms bent, on shoulders of *two*. From either a strong Eggbeater Kick or pushing from the bottom, *one* thrusts *two* feetfirst into a high Inverted Vertical

Figure 18.8.   Thrusting Flying Porpoise

position. The legs can be either together or in any other type of position variation. *Two* may then submerge headfirst in Inverted Vertical position, tuck and do a partial Somersault, or open legs in Scissors Split and finish as Walkover.

Thrusts or deep water lifts can also be done with Barracuda and other figure variations. Timing and position are most important. Each lift will require special positions of the hands, arms, and body as well as effective timing of the thrust. Experiment to find what works best for each lift. Practice!

Team Deep Water Lifts

Team deep water lifts can be accomplished if four or more swimmers adapt to deep water all of the lift techniques and positions described in this chapter.

In a team lift, one swimmer is usually lifted by the other team members. Because of the additional support of more than one swimmer, the lift can be sustained and more height obtained than in a deep water lift or thrust with just two people. Also, the team can be positioned in such a way to support lifts, such as Splits, that could not be accomplished without support on two sides.

Team deep water lifts are set into position underwater and then rise or thrust quickly into the lift itself. Thus the lift is very unexpected and can have a dynamic effect in a routine or composition.

The swimmers providing the most support should be positioned underneath, at the bottom of the lift, where they power-eggbeater and power-scull, using their shoulders or their backs to provide support for the swimmers above. The actual position and types of support that can be provided will depend on the type of lift, the number of swimmers involved, the amount of sustained height desired, and the type of position being held. Some lifts may require each of the swimmers providing support to do the same thing and be at the same level. Other lifts may involve some swimmers power-supporting other swimmers, who in turn will do the actual thrust or lift of the swimmer. By experimenting, you can achieve lifts that result in more than one swimmer being sustained either out of the water or in a higher position than could be achieved singly.

The best way to practice a team lift is to set the best pattern of support on deck, where swimmers can easily talk to each other and change positions, hand grips, and so on. Once the basic idea for the lift is created, set it to counts so that each person will be doing each movement at the same time. One or more counts should be for getting into general position, one or more counts for gripping and setting arms and legs into the base of support, and one or more counts for rising up toward the surface to the proper depth to execute the lift. Use one or more counts for setting and beginning a power Eggbeater Kick while the person (or persons) being lifted pre-pares to be lifted, one count for the actual lift, one or more counts for holding position, and one or more counts for submerging or whatever transition is used.

As with other lifts, the possibilities for new creations and ideas are unlimited, and once you begin creating, you will always be able to add to or change your creations to come up with even more innovative and exciting team lifts.

Chapter 19

Floating Patterns

Because of the large quantity of information available, floating patterns could well be the subject for a book. This chapter contains only the fundamentals, which you may use as a starting point to further explore this fascinating area of aquatic variations.

Floating patterns may be done by two or more persons. The more persons involved, the greater the variety of possible patterns and the greater the difficulty.

Technique Tips for Floating Patterns

1. Learn the basic connections used in floating pattern work first on land and then in shallow water.
2. Practice first by twos and then threes and more.
3. Stretch the entire body when forming patterns. It is particularly important to keep the knees, ankles, and insteps stretched and to point the toes to streamline the feet.
4. Make connections as secure as possible so that the pattern will not come apart. Do not use oil or grease on the body. Also, trim fingernails and toenails so that you and your partner will not scratch each other.
5. Whenever possible, *grip from underneath and exert pressure upward* to keep the pattern at the surface. If a foot or hand is placed on top, it should rest lightly and without weight. Even slight pressure downward can result in sinking the pattern.
6. Make your connections uniformly, inconspicuously, and as attractively as possible to avoid degrading or altering the line of the design.
7. Experiment to discover ways of activating or moving the pattern. If one or both arms are free, they may be used to stroke or scull. If the legs are free, they may be used for kicking. Even when arms and legs are not free, movement can result from opening and closing the arms, the

legs, or both. Some patterns may be moved in a straight line; others may turntable or move in a circular path.

8. Sculls, strokes, and figures are commonly used to change or move patterns. These movements include all standard strokes, Tub, Boat, Somersaults (partial and complete in Tuck and Pike positions), Oyster, Marlin, Waterwheel, Rolling, Planking, Shark, Dolphin, and Propeller.

9. Experiment to discover ways using as few movements as possible for getting into each pattern and changing from one pattern to another. Also explore the possibilities for varying each pattern.

Connections for Floating Patterns

Swimmers Side by Side, Facing Same Direction (Figure 19.1):

1. Clasp hands (A).
2. Grip with hand at wrist (B).
3. Grip with hand at elbow. This prevents elbow from bending (C).
4. Grip with hand at shoulder nearest you (D).
5. Grip with hand around waist (E).

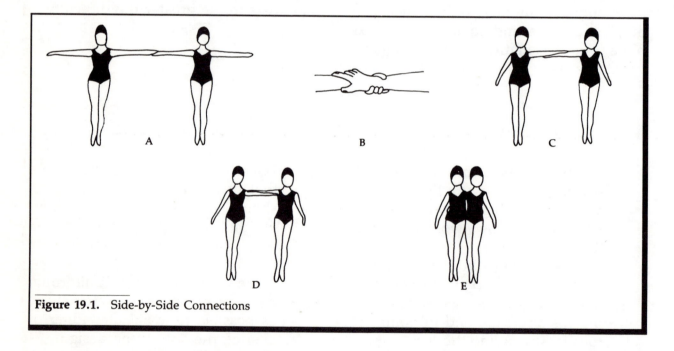

Figure 19.1. Side-by-Side Connections

Swimmers in Chain Formation, Head to Head (Figure 19.2):

1. Grip with hand at wrist (A).
2. Grip with hand at elbow (B).
3. Grip with hand at shoulder (C).

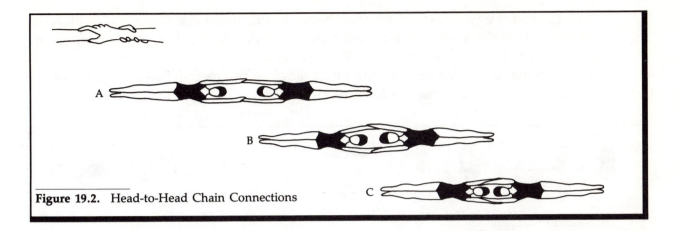

Figure 19.2. Head-to-Head Chain Connections

Swimmers Side by Side Facing in Opposite Directions (Figure 19.3):   Grip hands to feet, with hand underneath ball of foot. This connection is used in Accordion and Fan patterns.

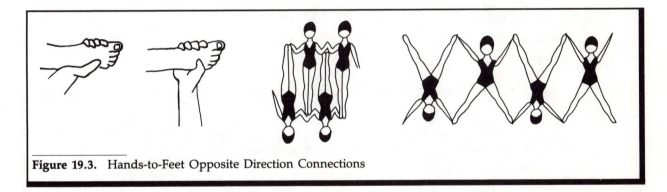

Figure 19.3. Hands-to-Feet Opposite Direction Connections

Swimmers in Chain Formation, All Facing Same Direction, Hands to Feet (Figure 19.4): This connection is also used in performing Planking. Grip with hand underneath ball or instep of foot. This results in a neater line than gripping underneath heel or ankle.

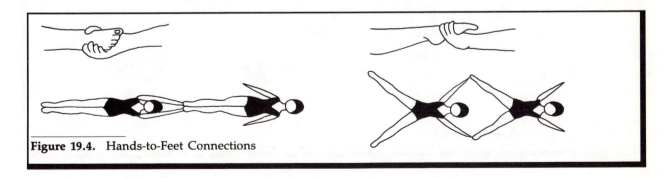

Figure 19.4. Hands-to-Feet Connections

Swimmers in Chain Formation, All Same Direction (Figure 19.5):

1. Feet to neck (A). On this connection do not toe in. Pressure may be exerted with the inner edges of the feet on the sides of the neck but not on the front of the

neck against the windpipe. Keep the heels down, point the toes, and stretch the ankles so that the arch of the foot fits over the shoulder. Do not exert any more pressure on the sides of the neck than necessary.

2. Feet to waist (B). Squeeze with the inner sides of the feet against the sides of the waist. Point the toes and stretch the ankles.

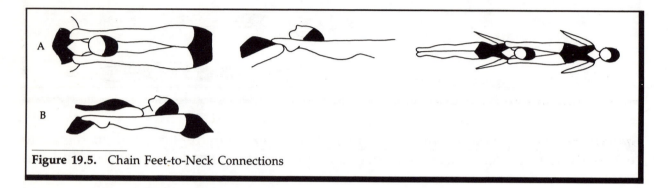

Figure 19.5. Chain Feet-to-Neck Connections

Swimmers in Chain Formation, Feet to Feet (Figure 19.6):

1. Interlock at ankles (A).
2. Interlock legs to just below knee level (B).

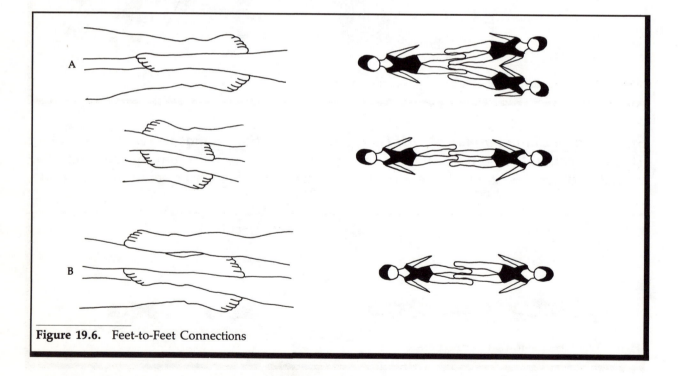

Figure 19.6. Feet-to-Feet Connections

Swimmers at Right Angles, Feet to Feet (Figure 19.7):   One swimmer connects to the other swimmer at ankles or instep, depending upon the pattern, by placing one foot underneath (press upward) and resting the other foot lightly (no weight) on top of the foot or ankle of the other swimmer. This connection is generally used in circle formations where the feet are in the center.

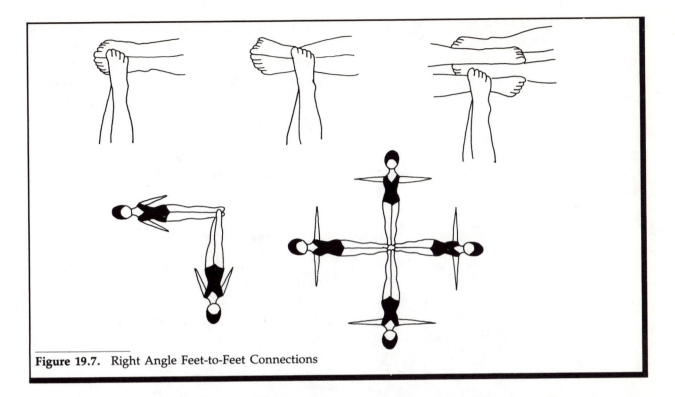

Figure 19.7. Right Angle Feet-to-Feet Connections

Swimmers in Stagger T Formation, Facing Same Direction (Figure 19.8): The top swimmer attaches feet to one arm of lower swimmer attaches feet to one arm of lower swimmer by placing one foot underneath (press upward) and resting the other foot lightly (no weight) on top of the arm of the other swimmer. The connection can be made at the wrist, forearm, elbow, or upper arm, depending upon the pattern.

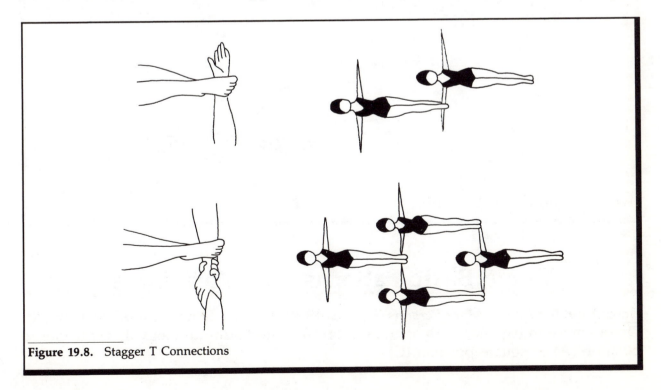

Figure 19.8. Stagger T Connections

Connections Used in Herringbone Pattern (Figure 19.9):   The center swimmer inserts an arm between the legs of the swimmer or swimmers at each side and clasps the inner surface of either leg, depending upon the movement to follow. The swimmers attached to the arms should squeeze their legs against the arm of the center swimmer. This connection is usually performed using three or more swimmers, with a swimmer on each arm of the center swimmer. The center swimmer may raise and lower the arms or move them to T position to create different designs. The swimmers attached to the arms may help by sculling with the arms at the sides, although the best way to perform Herringbone is with the attached swimmers keeping their arms tightly at their sides and not assisting with the propulsion.

> ### Technique Tips
> 1. The propulsion will be made easier if the attached swimmers hold their breath and keep a tight body during the movement.
> 2. When forming connections in which the legs are separated, do not separate the legs until it is absolutely necessary to do so. Opening the legs too soon results in an ugly line and a lack of neatness.

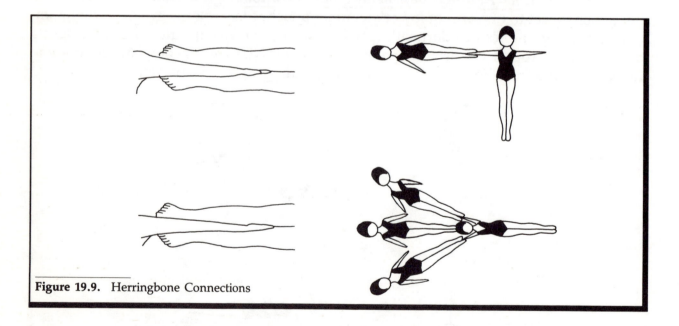

Figure 19.9. Herringbone Connections

Some Basic Patterns and Variations

Accordion, for Two or More Persons (Figures 19.10, 19.11):   Start in closed position (A). Open arms and legs slowly to open position (B). Close arms and legs slowly to closed position (A) or square position (C).

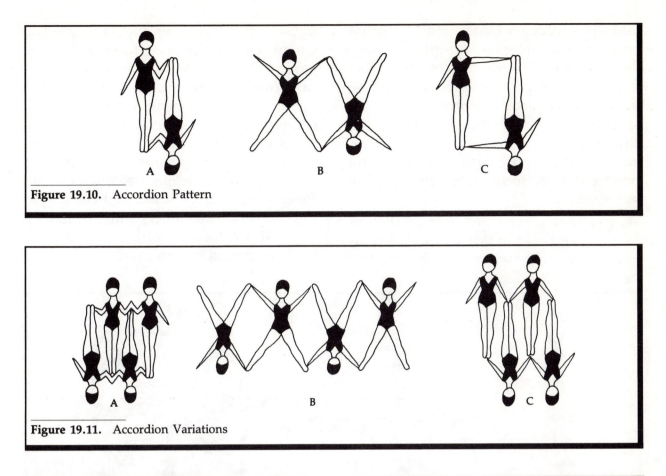

Figure 19.10. Accordion Pattern

Figure 19.11. Accordion Variations

Fan, for Three to Six Persons (Figure 19.12):
Start in closed Accordion. Swimmers *one*
and *three* open arms only. *Two* opens legs
only, to form a Fan. The pattern may be
reversed with *one* and *three* opening legs
and *two* opening arms.

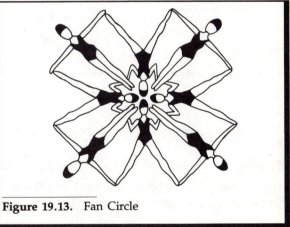

Figure 19.13. Fan Circle

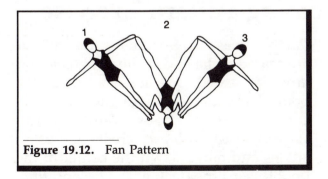

Figure 19.12. Fan Pattern

Fan Circle, for Eight Persons (Figure 19.13):
Open as in Fan. With eight persons, a
circle is formed and a connection made
when the circle is complete.

Anemone, for Eight Persons: This is a pattern that submerges and may rise again.
Make a Fan Circle. Swimmers on outside
of circle arch, pressing the legs down and
at the same time lifting the arms, while
center swimmers bend heads backwards
and close legs. This causes the pattern to

fold up; center swimmers sink headfirst and outer swimmers sink feetfirst, closing the formation. The effect is somewhat like that of a floating flower whose petals close up as the flower submerges. To be successful, the movements must be synchronized and performed with the same amount of force by each swimmer. The pattern may be surfaced by reversing the movements.

Wagon Wheel, for Eight Persons (Figure 19.14):   The Wagon Wheel is a circle pattern using eight swimmers with the feet

in the center. Two swimmers connect in Chain Formation, interlocking legs at ankles. Two swimmers then move in feetfirst (use Reverse Scull, body in Boat position) from opposite directions and connect to the interlocked feet of the first two swimmers by placing one foot below and one foot on top. Four more swimmers then move feetfirst into the circle between those already in position and connect to the center two swimmers with one foot on top and one foot underneath, as did the two swimmers before them.

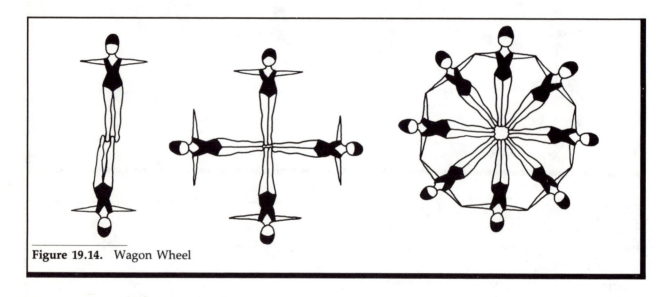

Figure 19.14.   Wagon Wheel

Designs for Four—A Floating Pattern Exercise

''Designs for Four''[1] includes an interesting variety of patterns as well as connections used frequently in floating pattern work. The counts and transition movements are suggestions, but others are possible. After learning the exercise, you should experiment and make changes. We hope that you will find ''Designs for Four'' helpful in learning and improving your floating pattern work and that it will inspire you to originate floating pattern compositions of your own.

(The following patterns are illustrated in Figure 19.15.)

Pattern One: (A) Swimmers *two* and *four* are seated at the end of the pool. *One* and *three* are seated, one at each side of the pool. Turn and slip into the water together, feetfirst (four counts, count slowly). *Two* and *four* chain ankles to ankles and move down the center of the pool toward the deep end. *One* and *three* move feetfirst, using Reverse Scull with the arms at the sides, and connect to *two*

---

[1]This floating pattern exercise was contributed by Verona Hiland, a former member of the Aquarelles of Cedar Rapids, Iowa. This material first appeared in *The Aquatic Art Book of Water Shows* (Gundling, 1964).

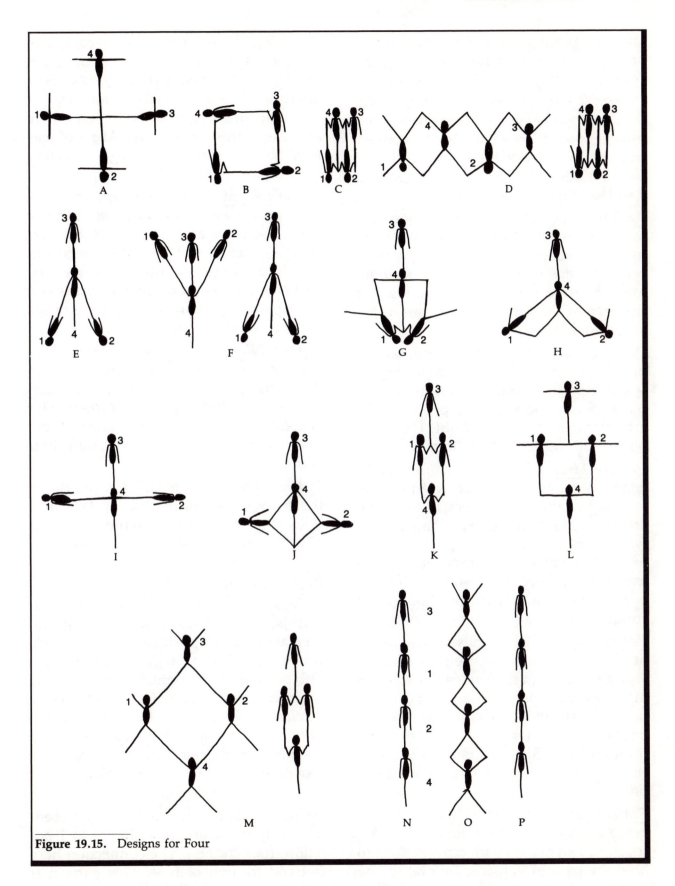

Figure 19.15. Designs for Four

and *four*, placing one foot under and one on top of the feet of *two* and *four* (eight counts). Hold pattern (four counts).

Pattern Two: (B) Break connection. All do Marlin to the right, making quarter turn (four counts). Make a hand-to-foot connection, elbows close to the side of the body, hands holding the arch of the foot so that a square pattern is formed (four counts).

Pattern Three: (C) Break connection. *One* and *three* stay in place. *Two* and *four* turntable in Tub position to the right (four counts). Move in to a closed position. Make hand-to-foot connections, holding the arch of the foot, elbows close to the sides (four counts).

Pattern Four: (D) Do Accordion. Slowly open arms and legs at the same time to V position (four counts). Perform movements slowly and exert even pressure. The arm movement is up and out. Hold pattern (four counts). Close (four counts).

Pattern Five: (E) Swimmer *three* breaks connection and moves backward behind *four* and chains feet to neck of *four*. *One* and *two* break connection and move backward slightly before moving into the arms of *four*. *Four* places her arms between the legs of *one* and *two*. The result is a Herringbone pattern in Down position (eight counts). Hold pattern (four counts).

Pattern Six: (F) *Four* raises arms overhead. *One* and *two* may help by sculling with their arms at their sides. *Three* sculls in place to hold pattern in the center of the pool. The result is a Herringbone pattern in the Up position (four counts). Hold (four counts). *Four* lowers arms to move *one* and *two* to Herringbone Down position (four counts).

Pattern Seven: (G) *Four* changes the leg grasp connection to hand to feet as in Accordion. *Three* sculls with arms at sides to hold the pattern in place. *Four* takes one foot of *one* and *two* and opens arms but keeps legs closed. *One* and *two* each take one foot of *four*, keeping elbows bent and arms close to the body (four counts). *Four* opens arms and *one* and *two* open legs at the same time (four counts). Open slowly and exert pressure evenly. Arms of *four* may be in T position or slightly down. Hold (four counts).

Pattern Eight: (H) Keep same connections and close the pattern. *One* and *two* close the legs, and *four* bends elbows, bringing the feet of *one* and *two* to her shoulders (four counts). Reverse the movement so *one* and *two* open arms and *four* opens legs (four counts). Legs of *one* and *two* remain closed.

Pattern Nine: (I) *One* and *two* break connection and *four* takes the connection for the Herringbone pattern with *one* and *two*. *Four* moves arms up to T position. *One* and *two* are attached to the arms of *four* with their legs (four counts). Hold (four counts).

Pattern Ten: (J) *One* slides r. leg down the body of *four* to the toes of *four*. *Two* does same movement with the l. leg. *Four* assists by moving her arms to a low V position (four counts).

Pattern Eleven: (K) Swimmer *four* lets go of legs of *one* and *two* with arms (four counts). *One* brings l. leg to r. leg and turntables in Tub position to the left while *two* brings r. leg to l. leg and turntables in Tub position to the right. *Three* breaks the chain connection and *four* moves slightly forward. With all facing in the same direction, move into a close position. *One* and *two* take one foot of *three*. *Four* takes one foot each of *one* and *two*. Keep elbows bent and close at sides (eight counts).

Pattern Twelve: (L) Keeping legs closed, all slowly move arm straight out to T position (four counts). The connection here is hand to arch of foot. This pattern is called a Pyramid. Hold (four counts).

Pattern Thirteen: (M) Slowly and all together, move the arms up to V position and at the same time open the legs (four counts). Be sure that the arms of *one* and *two* are in line with the legs of *three*. The arms of *four* should be in line with the legs of *one* and *two*. This is a Net pattern. Hold (four counts). Close the pattern to position described in K (four counts).

Pattern Fourteen: (N) Break connections. *One* and *three* move backward slightly while *two* and *four* move forward. All chain feet to neck to form a Chain pattern (four counts).

Pattern Fifteen: (O) Keep hands and elbows below the surface, reach up, and grasp underneath the feet on the neck. Slowly extend the arms straight up overhead, keeping the arms close to the head. Do not break the water surface on the extension of the arms (four counts). When the arms are extended overhead, slowly open the arms and legs to V position (four counts).

Pattern Sixteen: (P) Close arms and legs, arms overhead (four counts). Bring feet to neck as in Chain in N (four counts). Scull with the arms at the sides to move in chain pattern to the end of the pool for exit. Use Standard Scull to move headfirst, Reverse Scull to move feetfirst.

Floating Pattern Diagrams

The following floating pattern diagrams (Figure 19.16) were contributed by Katharina Jacobi, Damen Schwimm-Verein, Munich, Germany. These diagrams first appeared in *The Aquatic Art Book of Water Shows* (Gundling, 1964).

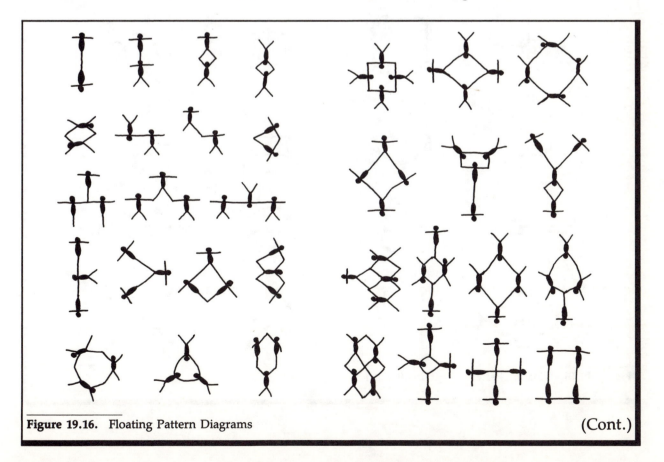

Figure 19.16. Floating Pattern Diagrams

(Cont.)

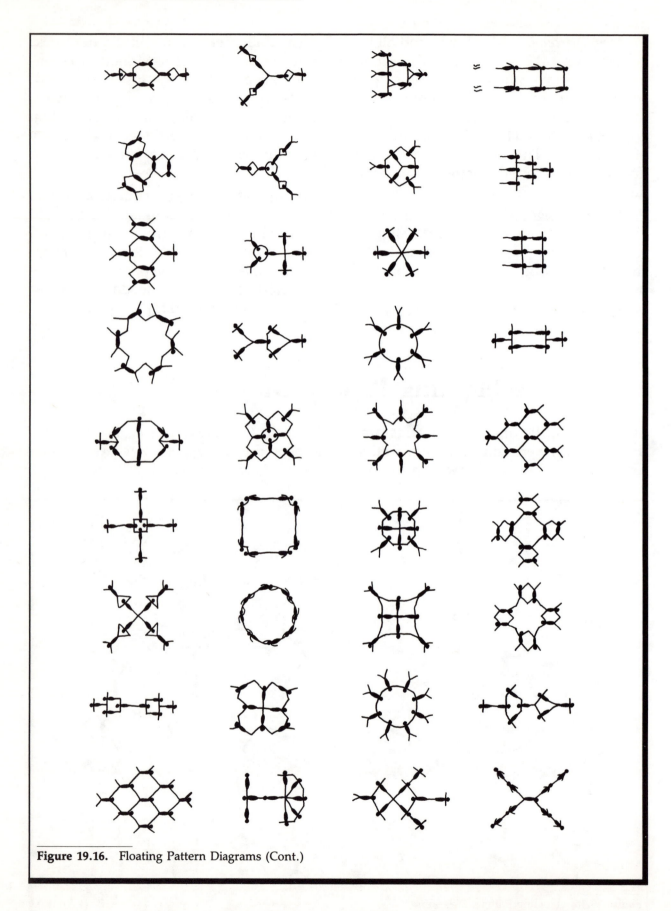

Figure 19.16.   Floating Pattern Diagrams (Cont.)

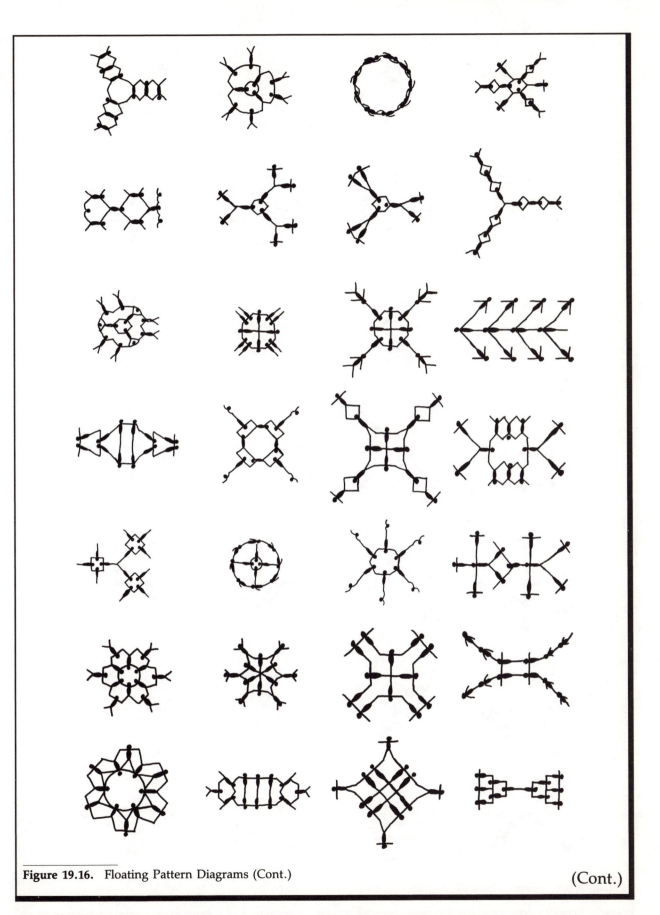

Figure 19.16. Floating Pattern Diagrams (Cont.)

(Cont.)

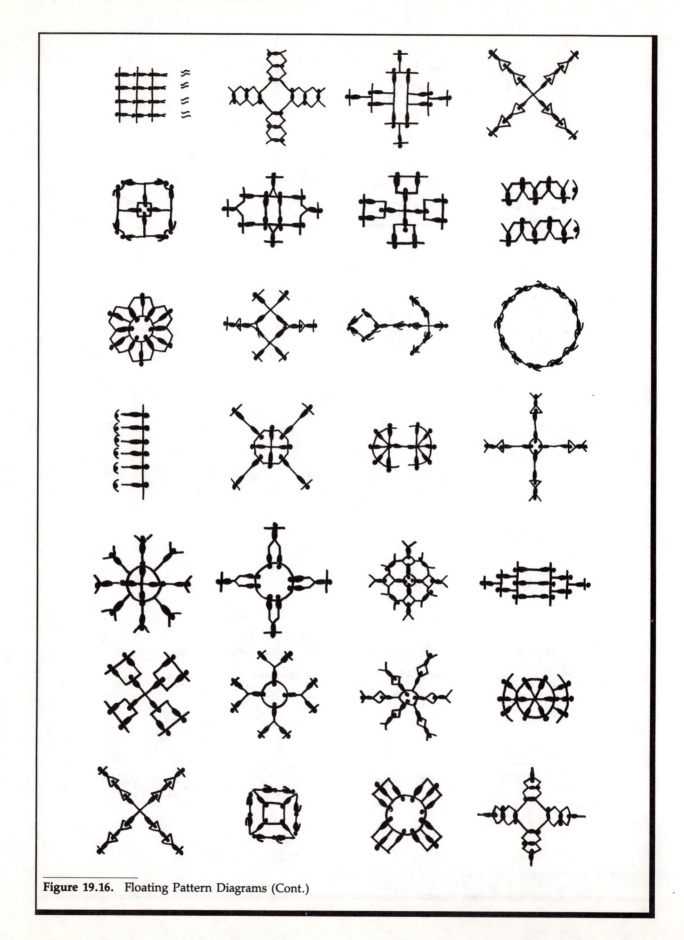

Figure 19.16. Floating Pattern Diagrams (Cont.)

Part IV
Fun With Warm-Ups and Technique Drills

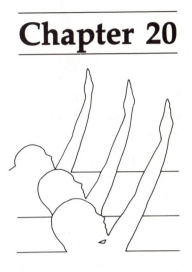

Warm-Ups

Chapter 20

Doing some type of warm-up exercises before practice or performance is always a good idea. Of course, warm-ups can be done on land—they frequently have to be, such as before a performance. Because a wealth of material on land exercises is available, there is no need to include it here. Instead, this chapter will focus on in-water exercises that are appropriate warm-ups and that can be used as lead-ups for learning skills.

You can do a variety of things in the water to warm up, such as swimming laps. However, these types of activities require lengths or widths of pool space, and because pool space for warm-ups is frequently limited, exercises that can be done in a very small area are especially useful.

Jumping Exercises

If space in shallow water (waist to shoulder depth) is available, these exercises are excellent. Jumping is one of the fastest ways of warming up the body, especially in cold water.

> **Technique Tips**
> 1. Bend knees over toes on landing.
> 2. Be sure heels contact bottom when completing landing and before starting the next jump.
> 3. Stretch entire body on jump.
> 4. Do not collapse on landing; keep back and head erect.

Jump and Scull (Figure 20.1):   Simply jump up and down, trying to get the body as high out of the water as possible. To give the arms exercise, do Standard Scull vigorously as you jump, trying to keep the body at its highest point in the jump for a few seconds longer than would be possible without sculling.

125

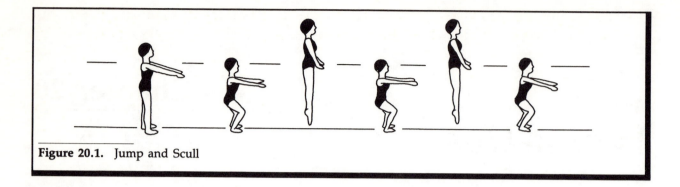

Figure 20.1. Jump and Scull

Swan Jump (Figure 20.2):   Stand with arms extended forward. Jump as high out of water as possible, raising arms overhead. At height of jump, open arms to V, arching body. Close arms and straighten body on descent. Repeat.

Jump and Turn: Jump three times in place and make one-half turn or more on the fourth jump. Repeat.

Figure 20.2. Swan Jump

Other Warm-Up Exercises

Ballet Exercises: If you study ballet, you will find that it is fun to use some of your ballet exercises in the shallow water as warm-ups for swimming. You can do Changements, Eschappes, Entrechats, or Soubresauts in various combinations.

Stationary Lobster (Figure 20.3):   This may be done in shallow or deep water. Perform Lobster but kick as hard as possible with the legs and scull as strongly as possible with the arms so that the body stays in place. If the legs are stronger, the body will move headfirst. If the arms are stronger, the body will move feetfirst. If you find yourself traveling, adjust accordingly. If done correctly, this warm-up strengthens both the leg kick and the scull.

Figure 20.3. Stationary Lobster

The Yo-Yo (Figure 20.4):   This warm-up was originated by Pat Haueter, South Milwaukee, Wisconsin. Hold onto pool edge as in A. Push vigorously away from pool wall, straightening arms and putting face in water so that the body moves feetfirst at the surface in Front Layout (B).

Before feetfirst momentum has decreased, begin Flutter Kicking vigorously so that the direction of movement is reversed and the body moves headfirst to the wall (C).

When hands touch wall, bend elbows and raise head (D). Inhale and repeat.

> **Technique Tips**
> 1. When kicking, bend wrists so palms face forward and make contact with the pool wall.
> 2. Try to return to pool wall as quickly as possible.
> 3. Streamline body after each push-off.
> 4. Breaststroke Kick may be used instead of Flutter Kick.

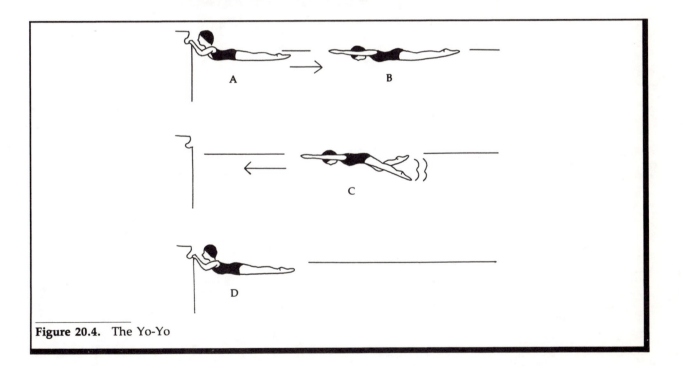

Figure 20.4.   The Yo-Yo

Seesaw Bobbing (Figure 20.5):   In addition to being fun, the Seesaw (when done correctly) is good exercise not only for warming up but also for strengthening arm and shoulder muscles, stretching the body, increasing lung capacity, and developing coordination.

In deep water face your partner and clasp hands. Alternately pull up and down with the arms so that one person sinks as the other person rises (head above the surface). Keep the body straight, legs together and stretched. Perform rhythmically (count 1: *one* up, *two* down; count 2: *one* down, *two* up; etc.).

Experiment doing the Seesaw (a) using various depths of water, (b) varying the amount of force used on the arm pulls, and (c) changing the body position so that the body tucks when rising and straightens when sinking, or vice versa.

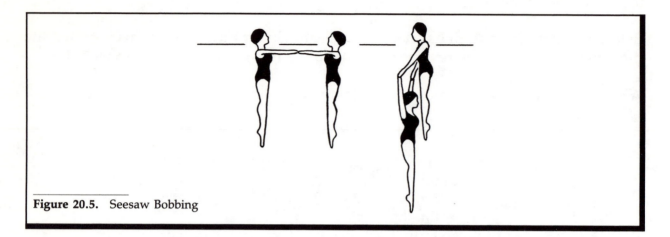

Figure 20.5.   Seesaw Bobbing

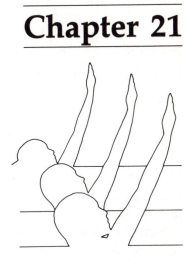

Chapter 21

Tips for Improving Technique

In a sense, all figures, strokes, and variations can be considered exercises because they develop various muscles if they are done correctly. This type of exercise can improve strength, endurance, flexibility, and coordination, thus increasing your skill and enjoyment in the water. This chapter includes exercises that are specific to certain movements and that are designed to correct common technique faults.

Keeping Legs Together

One of the most common faults is letting the legs drift apart when they should be held tightly together. This usually happens when you lose concentration.

To help you remember to keep the legs together, take a flat piece of plastic, such as a plastic lid from a can, and place it between your feet.

Practice the following figures while firmly holding the plastic: Boat, Tub, Somersaults, Marlin, Shark, Double Ballet Legs, Dolphin, Kip, Porpoise, and Barracuda. Practice other figures in which the legs remain together throughout. Frequent practice with a piece of plastic or some similar object will be of great help in eliminating this common fault.

Figure 21.1. Keeping Legs Together

Using Balls to Correct Head Position

Small balls are helpful in correcting head positions in Inverted positions. For example, use a Ping-Pong ball held under the chin to practice such figures as Kip and Porpoise. The ball is especially useful for swimmers who have a habit of raising the head and arching the back when inverted. Using small balls of other assorted sizes is helpful in practicing figures in which the head should be forward.

Surface Tuck and Stretch Exercise

Place kickboard so that it is in contact with legs from the toes to knees and stretch to Boat position (Figure 21.2, A). Slowly and smoothly assume Tub (B) and tight Tuck (C), keeping the board level and just above the surface so it will not float away. Slowly and smoothly reverse the movements. Use Flat Scull to stay in place and for lifting power to keep the feet high enough at the surface to support the board.

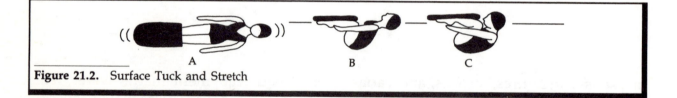

Figure 21.2. Surface Tuck and Stretch

Changing From Pike to Inverted Vertical

The following exercise will help you get the feel of uncoiling and coiling necessary for some figures and variations.

Place legs over the side of the pool as shown in Figure 21.3 (A) and clasp hands behind head. Slowly straighten body to Inverted Vertical, keeping knees bent and hands clasped behind head (B). *Do not arch*. Reverse the movements to return to the surface. Repeat.

Technique Tips
1. The hands are clasped behind the head (a) to protect it in case you do not do the exercise correctly and (b) to make the muscles of the trunk do the work instead of depending on the arms.
2. Uncoil starting at the base of the spine; make the head the last part of the body to come into vertical alignment.
3. In reversing, the coiling up starts with the head.
4. Perform slowly and smoothly.

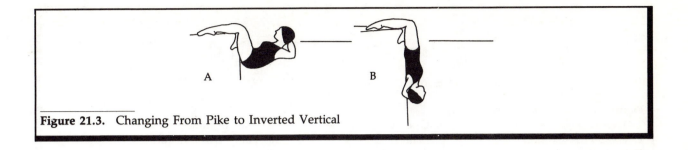

Figure 21.3. Changing From Pike to Inverted Vertical

Basic Sculling

One of the secrets for expert execution of many figures and floating patterns is the ability to scull well. Proper sculling helps you achieve continuous, smooth propulsion using only the arms. In addition, sculling allows you to balance and support the body in positions that would be impossible to maintain by any other means. Sculling also provides lifting power and enables you to move the body smoothly and gracefully in a great variety of positions and in practically any direction. It is used within figures to aid in holding a position, in surfacing, or in submerging.

The following technique tips for improving basic sculling are based on the system of sculling instruction developed by Mr. George Gordon Hyde (cited in Gundling, 1966). Mr. Hyde, a pioneer in the technical analysis of sculling based on the principles of physics, was the first to develop a complete system of instruction and has contributed greatly to aquatic art and the sport of synchronized swimming.

The following points should be kept in mind when learning, practicing, and perfecting basic sculling:

1. Keep hands flat, fingers together.
2. Arms move sideways from shoulders. Elbows may be straight throughout or bent on the inward movement for more power.
3. The range of movement is relatively small. The arms move out to low V position and in toward sides of body if in Boat position; arms move toward median line of body if they are overhead as in Propeller (Torpedo) and Lobster.
4. Palms are angled slightly so that little finger edge is raised on outward movement and thumb edge is raised on inward movement.
5. Palm angle is changed quickly at *end* of each inward and outward movement of the arms so that *continuous pressure* is exerted on the water by the palms. To exert pressure, the palm must be angled or tilted, rather than merely slicing through the water. To determine the amount of palm angle necessary for efficient sculling, place the hand, palm down, on a flat surface and tilt it so that one edge of the hand rests on the flat surface and the other edge is about one inch above the surface. Practice raising first one edge then the other edge of the hand.
6. If the body is in a prone position at the surface, the arms scull just below the surface.

Learning to Scull

First, practice sculling movements on land using floor, wall, or other flat surface.

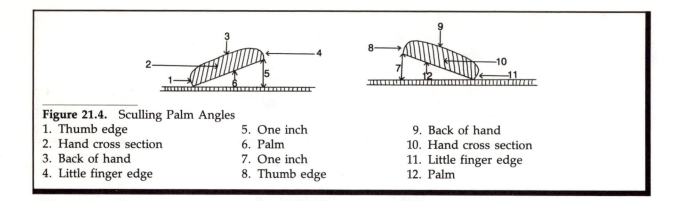

Figure 21.4. Sculling Palm Angles

1. Thumb edge	5. One inch	9. Back of hand
2. Hand cross section	6. Palm	10. Hand cross section
3. Back of hand	7. One inch	11. Little finger edge
4. Little finger edge	8. Thumb edge	12. Palm

Then practice while standing in shallow water until technique is learned. Next, scull with body in Boat, Tub, and Lobster positions. As strength and skill are acquired, practice Propeller, Canoe, and Sailboat. When Sailboat can be done correctly, go on to Ballet Leg and variations. Then work on Double Ballet Leg.

Support Scull Exercises

Support Scull is an advanced technique used to maintain the body at as high a level as possible in Inverted Vertical positions. It is similar to Bent Arm Flat Scull performed with the body in a Vertical Head-Out position, except that the palms face *up* instead of down. Figure 21.5 illustrates the positions described in Exercises One Through Five.

Exercise One: Stand on land, arms bent as in A. *Angle the palms so that the little finger edge is slightly higher.* Keeping the arms bent approximately at a right angle, move the arms out as shown in B (front view). Return the arms to position shown in A but *change the palm angle so that the thumb edge of the hand is slightly higher* on the return movement. Do the movements slowly, checking to be certain they are correct.

Technique Tips

1. Keep wrists and palms flat, fingers together.
2. Hold the body very erect.
3. On the outward movement of the arms, feel the shoulder blades moving toward each other and the chest expanding. Relax these muscles on the inward movement but don't slump or round the back.
4. Keep the bend at the elbows approximately a right angle—avoid an acute angle.
5. Practice with a book or light weight on each palm to give you the feeling of pressure against the water.

Exercise Two: Do Support Scull while standing in chest to shoulder depth water. Be sure to feel the pressure of the water on the palms of the hands during both the outward and inward movements.

Exercise Three: In water that is about a foot over your head, assume a Vertical position and do Support Scull (C). If you are doing the movements correctly and with sufficient power, the body will move smoothly feetfirst to the bottom, and the Support Scull will keep your feet firmly on the bottom until you want to surface (D). When you can do this without difficulty, practice in deeper water.

Exercise Four: When you can do Exercise Three easily and well, try the Support Scull with the body inverted. Despite all the preliminary work you have done, you are apt to find everything totally different once you are upside down. First try the Support Scull in positions in which the

body can float with little or no help from the arms, such as Inverted Tuck, Inverted Spearfish, or a very wide Scissors Split. Practicing the Support Scull in these positions is to accustom you to supporting yourself in an upside-down position, rather than to raise up the body unusually high (E).

Exercise Five: Practice Support Scull with the body in Fishtail position and in Inverted Vertical Bent Knee position (F).

Figure 21.5. Support Scull Exercises

Technique Tips for Support Scull

1. You may notice that some adjustments must be made in the scull when the body and the legs are in different positions.
2. There is more support and lifting power if the hands are fairly close to the surface in the hip area.
3. The farther the hands get above waist level, the less power they have for raising and supporting the body.
4. Keep the body straight—do not pike or arch.
5. When assuming an Inverted Vertical position in which you plan to use Support Scull, extend the body smoothly and easily to the Inverted Vertical—do not thrust forcefully.
6. Concentrate initially on smoothness and control, rather than on height.

Exercises for the Cut-Through (Sometimes Called the Catch)

The Cut-Through is a technique by which the arms are brought into position for the Support Scull. If you wish to sustain the height of the body when it reaches the Inverted Vertical position, the hands must Cut-Through to the position for Support Scull. Practice this on land and while standing in chest-deep water.

Bend forward, arms extended backward as shown in Figure 21.6, A. Do Flat Scull while slowly straightening the body (B). Just before the body is completely erect and the arms have moved outward while sculling, bend the elbows, bringing hands in (palms facing up), fingertips toward the sides of the body at the waist (C). Extend the arms forward to Support Scull position (D), and *immediately* begin Support Scull.

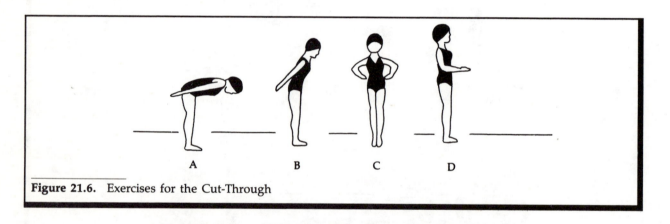

Figure 21.6. Exercises for the Cut-Through

Technique Tips

1. Timing is very important. By experimenting you will discover the best point at which to make the Cut-Through.
2. When using the Cut-Through on a figure such as Barracuda, do not at first try for great height. Rather than thrusting, move slowly up into the Inverted Vertical position.
3. A Bent Knee Inverted Vertical position is easier to control than one with legs together.
4. Begin sculling as soon as the arms come into position for Support Scull.

Analysis of Basic Layout Postures

Many errors and difficulties in performing aquatic skills are related to the posture of the body in the water. Correct posture and alignment are essential for the skill being performed. The following analysis of postures was developed by Marian Ruch of Stanford University (cited in Gundling, 1964).

In this discussion, the term "posture" refers to the total alignment of those segments of the body which are not involved in the movements of propulsion or support. In the Dolphin, for instance, this would include everything except the arms. The posture, or course, might change several times within the execution of a single figure.

The basic aquatic postures are the layout, the tuck, and the pike. These main classes can be subdivided into various categories. This article is concerned only with layout postures. These may be subdivided into the "straight layout position," the "arched layout position," and the "contracted layout position." A swimmer who learns the "feel" and control of these three postures will not only improve his performance, but also will be able to analyze and master new skills more readily.

The straight layout is described first because it is the neutral position and similar to good standing posture. However, the contracted layout position should be mastered first for it is used in such basic skills as Boat and horizontal floating. There is a whole continuum of layout postures between the extremes of the contracted and the arched positions. The amount of arch or contraction used will vary, not only with the nature and speed of the stroke or figure, but with the body structure of the performer.

The Straight Layout Position

Except for the rigidly extended ankles, knees, and hips, a description of standing posture will describe the straight layout position. The body segments are in a straight line: the pelvis is tilted up toward crown of head in front and down toward soles of feet in back; the lumbar spine (low back) has a normal, mild concavity; the abdomen is flat; the chest is slightly elevated; the neck is straight; the eyes look straight ahead.

The straight layout position is used as the body descends in a dive, such as the plain front dive, Porpoise, Kip, etc. It is also used in those figures which require twisting in the vertical position.

The straight layout position is difficult to master in the inverted vertical position because of the natural tendency to throw the head backward to look at the bottom of the pool for orientation. This tendency not only destroys the straight alignment of the segments, but usually causes the low back to arch unduly in order to maintain balance. The swimmer should learn to look at the side wall and to "unarch" the lumbar spine. It is true that some performers can bend the head backward to look at the bottom of the pool and still keep the rest of the body straight. However, if the body is to twist about a vertical axis, then the central axis of each main body segment should lie in a straight line which coincides with the axis of rotation. Segments which are out of line will move in circles about the vertical axis. For example, when the back is arched during a twist, the toes move in a circle rather than a true twist about an axis passing through all segments from the top of the head to the tips of the toes.

In a twist it is possible to look at the bottom without throwing the head out of line if the head is tilted so that the ear lobes are kept in the vertical line of the body segments so that the balance will not be disturbed. The secret is this—the center of gravity of the head is approximately in line with the ear lobes.

The Inverted Vertical position is a bugbear to many swimmers not because it is actually difficult, but because the sensation is quite different from anything encountered in ordinary activities. If the segments are really aligned vertically, one over the other, it takes practically no effort to balance the body since gravity cannot tip the body unless it is out of the vertical line. As a matter of fact, one can float in this inverted position with the feet out of the water if he can achieve this balanced position and let the water support him. Many swimmers waste energy trying to maintain balance with compensatory arm movements or strained postures instead of arranging the body segments so that the forces of gravity and buoyancy act together to balance and support the body in the desired position. This is true not only in the vertical and inverted position, but in all positions.

The Contracted Layout Position

This posture is used in the back float, Boat, and sculling on the back. This posture plays two important functions in the backlying position. First, it keeps the body horizontal; second, it streamlines the back, or "keel," of the body so that it can glide straight through the water with grace and speed.

The amount of contraction required depends not only upon the technique being performed, but upon the buoyancy and the body structure of the performer. The following description is of the *exaggerated* contracted layout position as it might be taught to a novice or a person with little natural buoyancy. Each individual must experiment with his own posture in the water to determine the exact pelvic and neck positions which he needs to keep his body horizontal and streamlined.

In the exaggerated contracted layout position, the neck is "hyperstraight" and is pressed firmly backward without tilting the head backward. The chin is *slightly* down; the back of the head and the back of the neck rest in the water.

The normal forward-upward tilt of the pelvis is exaggerated by a strong abdominal contraction. This "sucking in" of the abdomen also flattens the normal lumbar curve to the straight line or even reverses it slightly so that the low back is mildly rounded (this depends upon the flexibility of the individual). The buttocks are tightly contracted to press the hips forward and to prevent any tendency to "pike." The upper back and chest remain in the normal position as the spine, as a whole, assumes a smooth, flat C curve by eliminating the normal concavities in the lumbar and cervical (neck) regions.

The effect of this posture in holding the body in a horizontal position can best be illustrated by the back float. Many individuals who insist that they cannot float horizontally on the back can do so if they will only master the contracted layout position. The extreme tilt of the pelvis raises the straight legs to the surface, and the stretch of the head and the neck rotates the body, as a whole, from the diagonal to the horizontal position. The rigid body is like a seesaw rotating about its axis, which, in this case, is the center of gravity of the body. Each person must experiment with his own pelvic and head positions until he finds his balance point. It should be emphasized that this is not a "dead" float but an "active" one. Most persons who become aware of the kinesthetic "feel" of the position can float with very little muscular tension, but they must be alert to any tendency of the feet to drop and readjust the head or pelvic positions to keep the body horizontal.

If the feet sink in spite of a strong pelvic tilt, the swimmer should stretch the back of the neck and press his ears toward the bottom of the pool, being sure not to tilt the head backward. Persons who have difficulty in learning this float may extend their arms on the water overhead and, if necessary, flex the wrists to bring the hands out of water. After they learn to float in this position, they can usually bring the arms to V and T positions. Any person who can float horizontally on his face can do so on his back if he will only make up his mind to do it and experiment until he masters the control of the body segments, mainly the pelvic and head-neck segments.

In Boat, the contracted layout position is important to keeping the feet, legs, and hips on the surface, as well as streamlining the body. If the hands

scull at the sides they will assist in keeping the body on the surface, but if the hands are overhead as in Propeller, it becomes the function of the buttock and abdominal muscles to keep the hips on the surface and the feet pointed in the direction of motion. Again, each person must experiment to determine the degree of muscle tension which he must exert to maintain good posture for the particular skill being performed.

The Arched Layout Position

The thoracic spine is normally slightly convex in back. A strong contraction of the upper back extensors will straighten this curve and lift the chest. The cervical and lumbar curves are already concave, and these concavities can be readily increased by contraction of the back muscles.

The problem in the arched layout position is to avoid overarching in the cervical and lumbar regions. To counteract this tendency, the swimmer should concentrate on arching the upper back. This is anatomically impossible, but a strong extension of the upper back, with a lift of the chest "feels" like an arch of the upper back. The chin is raised slightly and the neck pressed back, but the head is not thrown all the way back, except perhaps in teaching the Dolphin to beginners. The lumbar region is arched only enough to make a smooth, curved line with the rest of the spine. Overarching here is controlled by contracting the abdominal muscles.

Overarching is probably one of the most common errors in the execution of dives and inverted vertical figures. It is important to remember that hyperextension of the hip joint is anatomically impossible. When the legs overthrow in a front header or in a Porpoise, it is not a matter of hyperextension of the hips, but hyperextension of the lumbar spine. This must be prevented by contraction of the abdominal muscles, not the hip flexors. Contraction of the hip flexors will cause the body to pike.

Overarching frequently occurs in Dolphin when the swimmer does not go deep enough, when he throws his head too far back, or when he attempts to throw himself backward by ''arching into'' the figure rather than pulling himself around with the arms. It might be well to note here that in smooth execution of figures, the postural muscles are used to control the ''line'' of the body as required for the particular figure, *not to move the body*. This is the job of the arms or legs, depending upon the figure. In a controlled back arch, the alignment of the body forms a smooth curved line. Some figures, such as Swordfish, require more arch than others, but the tendency to overarch in the cervical and lumbar regions of the body should be kept to a minimum not only to preserve the beauty of the line of the body, but to avoid strain of the very vulnerable low back. (pp. 131-136).

Part V
Fun With Performing and Creating

Keys to Successful Performing

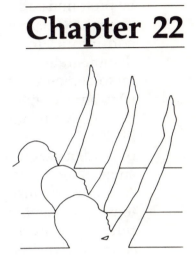

Although the primary purpose of this book is to increase your enjoyment of the water through variations of aquatic skills, some information on performing should be included. Even if your purpose in learning aquatic skills is for fun and not because you aspire to be an aquatic artist or synchronized swimming champion, you may have opportunities to take part in water shows and exhibitions given by your club, school, or other organization.

If you perform, you have a responsibility to your audience. You can do so much more with a simple skill once it is developed into a *performing art*. You then have the opportunity to use the medium of water in the same way other artists use different mediums—the dancer uses land, the ice skater uses ice, and the thespian uses the stage. Our medium holds so many exciting avenues for artistic expression that are not available to any other performer. Use and explore them!

In a performing art, all movements must be performed not only expertly but also with feeling. Expressive movement comes *after* execution is mastered. In turn, mastery of execution comes from *first* building a strong foundation on the basic skills. Often, performers get so excited and involved with the performing and creating that they do not spend enough time developing the strong base of basic skills. Please do not lose sight of the fact that the well-executed skill is what makes creative expression possible. Practice, practice, practice! Your technical skills must be so excellent that you are free to concentrate on communication through movement.

If you decide to perform, first ask yourself the following questions and answer them honestly.

1. What is my purpose in performing? A performer should have a legitimate and specific purpose for performing. Performing for no specific

reason, or merely to show off, simply wastes the time of the audience. The purpose does not have to be profound and may be (a) to demonstrate execution, (b) to educate and inform, (c) to astound, (d) to demonstrate your improvement, (e) to demonstrate synchronization, (f) to amuse or entertain, (g) to portray or give an interpretation, (h) to lift up the spirits, (i) to reveal new or hidden beauties or truth in some subject, or (j) to increase understanding and insight. Often the intent is a combination of several purposes. Every performer, of course, demonstrates execution, and execution must be of high quality to convey the purpose and the theme. However, technique in an art form is only the servant, not the master. Originate and plan your composition around your purpose. It is often a good idea to put it in writing; this will help fix it clearly and securely in your mind.

2. What are my capabilities? You must have the technical capability to execute well the movements in the composition. The movements you choose must be performed with such technical excellence that you are free to concentrate on communication of movement. Challenge yourself to master difficult skills but do not incorporate them into a composition until they are learned and well practiced. Doing a simple movement well and with expression will give both you and the audience more satisfaction than doing difficult skills poorly. Stay within the range of your ability when performing in public, no matter how small or limited that range may be.

3. How am I going to accomplish my objectives? *Plan* and *schedule* your practice times, rehearsal performances, costume design, music taping, and all the details involved in preparing to present yourself to best advantage before an audience. Don't leave your preparation to chance—if you know you are well prepared, you will have the added confidence to give your best performance every time.

Performing can be fun, but it can also be frightening, particularly at first. Nevertheless, it can be one of the most rewarding and satisfying activities you can do—for yourself and your audience. The following pointers (in alphabetical order) will help you develop the trademarks of a skilled performer.

Accompaniment and Choreography

Even the most skilled performer cannot rise above mediocre choreography and accompaniment. Remember, the finest music in the world is available to accompany your performance. If you can have jewels, why take glass? Choreography and accompaniment should be in harmony, and each should enhance the other. Both should be of superior quality if a performance is to be outstanding.

Keep your performance short; the spectators will feel that they would like to see more. It is also very important that you really like your accompaniment and composition. Then practice and performance will not be drudgery but a pleasure.

Concentration

Concentration is all-important. Distractions can cause you to make mistakes and to have momentary (or longer) lapses of memory; in any case, they prevent you from doing your best. Although some distractions (such as problems with the sound equipment, unexpected noises) are beyond your control, others are not.

Before performing, prepare yourself by walking through your composition on land and/or thinking through it carefully from beginning to end, hearing your accompaniment in your imagination. This is difficult to do if you are hearing the music for another number, so try to find a quiet place.

Fix in your mind the impression that you would like to convey to the audience. You must picture this as vividly and accurately as possible—a hazy view is hardly useful. Think of the mood, the message, and the meaning of your composition.

Try to allow a few moments, at least, for quiet reflection and deep breathing before you make your appearance. Chattering with the other performers is fine while you are waiting, but allow yourself sufficient time to get in character. This can't be done as quickly and easily as turning on and off a faucet. Moreover, missing or almost missing your cue gets you off to a bad start.

Cultivate the on-stage ability to concentrate on the theme of your composition. This will make you oblivious to many of the petty disturbances and unfavorable conditions that may exist.

When performing, do not wonder what impression you are making on the spectators. Forget about them. Instead, focus on what you are doing. Enjoy the sensation of performing expressive, rhythmic aquatic movements in harmony with your accompaniment.

If you have trained yourself to concentrate during practice, concentrating while performing will be easier.

Confidence

Confidence is not to be confused with cockiness or conceit. Confidence comes from knowing that you are thoroughly prepared. It is built up through practice—not wishful thinking—and through experience in performing.

With practice you know you are capable of doing what you want to do in performance. With experience in performing you learn to adapt to different conditions and situations, to overcome, or at least to compensate for unfavorable ones.

The result is that you become a poised, skilled performer in complete control of the situation from the moment you are on stage.

Costuming

Appropriate costuming can add to your enjoyment and to that of the spectators. Skillfully using color and design in your costuming can assist you in expressing the theme of your composition and conveying it to the spectators.

An appropriate costume is becoming, comfortable, and simple. Avoid elaborate costumes that may hamper movement and detract from your performance.

Criticism

If you do not want criticism of your work, performing is not for you, for when you perform, every person who is watching becomes a critic and forms an opinion of your work. In general, the knowledge of spectators usually ranges from knowing little or nothing about what you are doing (this does not keep them from criticizing) to having a good understanding of an aquatic performance. In addition, there are

usually some fault-finding individuals who look only for flaws (they naturally find or invent some), and at the other extreme there are people who think everything the performer does is wonderful. As a result, you must learn to take both praise and critical remarks gracefully. Accept and benefit from constructive criticism and disregard that which is not.

Elegance

The skilled performer has refinement, grace, and propriety. Everything that is

cheap, vulgar, offensive, or in poor or questionable taste is totally absent.

Facial Expression

Avoid fixed, feigned, or phony facial expressions, as well as those bearing no relationship to your composition. Some persons have the idea that performers should smile all the time because this constitutes good showmanship. However, the facial expression should reflect the feeling expressed by the composition. If a composition is happy, a smile is appropriate, but if the composition is serious, a wide grin is entirely out of place.

Whatever the facial expression, it should not be forced or superficially assumed, but, instead, it should come from within. Effective and appropriate expression of the face and body comes from repeated, thoughtful practice of a composition, which allows you to inwardly experience its moods and emotions.

Humility

The worst thing that can happen to any performer is to become egotistical and inflated with self-importance. Such a person is unpopular with the public and with the other performers as well. With the loss of humility, ability declines because the conceited performer—although critical of others—is blind to his or her own faults and thus has no incentive to improve. The humble performer realizes that it is always possible to improve and continually strives to do so.

Keeping Fit

It is impossible to do your best if you are not feeling up to par. So it is important to keep fit with the three basics: exercise, diet, and rest.

If you swim regularly and frequently, you probably get sufficient exercise. But equally important are a nutritious diet and adequate rest and relaxation.

In addition, it is a good idea both to perform and to practice on an empty stomach. Otherwise digestive problems can prevent you from doing your best, as well as rob you of the pleasure you should receive from swimming.

Mistakes

Mistakes are inevitable. However, those due to lack of practice or the result of attempting skills beyond your ability can be eliminated—the former by more practice, the latter by only using movements in your compositions that you can do easily.

Some mistakes may be caused by the tensions of performing or by things beyond your control. What should you do if you make a mistake during performance? Don't panic. The best thing to do is to erase it immediately from your mind and continue as if nothing had happened. If you don't advertise your mistake, chances are the spectators may not notice it. But what if you really mess things up? Well, it is not the end of the world, and the spectators are usually sympathetic toward a performer who makes an obvious error and handles it with poise.

The important thing is to learn from your mistake. After any performance, it is always a good idea to review and analyze it. What went well? What didn't? Why? What do I need to work on to improve? By pinpointing the cause of problems, you can work on correcting them.

On Stage

Remember, if you are in view of the spectators, you are on stage even though you have not started or have finished your performance. Adjustments of costume, talking, or displays of emotion that are not part of your composition should be done in an area not visible to any spectators. If you can be seen by anyone, be at your professional best.

Practice

There is no substitute for the right kind of practice. The best choreography, accompaniment, costuming, and personal charm and beauty cannot make up for lack of it. Too many swimmers appear in public without adequate prior practice of their compositions. They may spend so many hours on items such as costuming and makeup that they have little time left for practicing the composition before the performance. The results are all too evident.

For practice to be effective, practice carefully, not carelessly. Avoid distractions and interruptions as much as possible. Think about what you are doing and do not let your mind wander. Pay attention to details, no matter how minute, because each is important to the total effect. Also remember to practice your underwater skills. You are not invisible when you submerge, so pay attention to keeping your underwater movements neat and to a minimum. First and last impressions are also particularly important, so give special attention to these parts of the performance.

Preperformance Butterflies

Even the most experienced performers experience some nervousness before performing, so if you have the feeling of butterflies in your stomach, you are not alone. Here are some suggestions that can slow down the fluttering:

1. Knowing that you are well-prepared can give you assurance—a feeling of being in control.

2. Before performing, deep breathing, relaxation, and stretching movements can be beneficial. If the water and air are cold, do warm-up exercises such as jogging in place, arm swings, and so on.
3. Walk through your composition in the locker room or visualize it vividly in your mind.

Sincerity

You must feel with sufficient intensity the theme or mood you wish to express if you are to convey this to others. You must like and believe in your composition. If you are merely executing a series of movements in a technically skillful manner, the result will be a cold, mechanical performance.

Instead, the movements must be performed with the feeling that comes from within you. All pretense and artificiality should be completely cast out. Sham is easily spotted by the spectators, but the person who is natural and sincere captivates them.

Sincerity requires mental and emotional effort on your part. You must probe into yourself and discover what you are capable of expressing.

Sound Equipment

Problems with the sound equipment can mar or even destroy your performance and are usually beyond your control. Yet, as a performer, you can avoid some of these difficulties by making certain the recording of the accompaniment of your composition is of good quality, properly labeled, and preferably the first and only selection on the tape.

You or your coach should give the sound operator specific instruction concerning correct volume, when to start the music, where you will make your entrance, where you will be performing deckwork and entry into the water, and when the composition is finished.

Of course, persons in charge of a performance should do their best to obtain high quality sound equipment and, equally important, a capable operator.

To Give and to Receive

As a performer you can both give and receive if you have the right attitude. If you think of performing as giving, of the spectators as recipients, you will discover that you are a recipient as well.

If you are to be both a giver and a receiver, performing should never be done to show off by trying to impress others with your ability, charm, or beauty. Neither should it be done to show up the other performers by trying to display your superiority.

Also, performing should be more than a mere display of your skill. Instead, you should present something you feel will be of value, or at least of interest, to others—a sharing with them of your enjoyment of aquatic movement, your interpretation of the theme and accompaniment of your composition.

Think of performing as a gift—a gift to the spectators—and just as you would want any other gift you would give to someone you like to be of the best quality, so in creating and in performing a composition, you should want it to be the best you are capable of at the time.

This means you must be willing to take the time and to exert the effort required to make it so. Then you will enjoy the pleasure of giving and the spectators will enjoy your gift.

Trademarks of a Skilled Performer

All skilled performers can be singled out by their command of the following abilities.

1. *The illusion of ease.* The illusion of ease comes only with much practice.

2. *A sense of timing.* The timing of the composition as a whole, the timing of the movements within the accompaniment, the timing of the entrance, the ending, the bow—all of these must be just right if the performance is to be effective.

3. *Responsiveness to music.* The music should provide a stimulus for movement and should affect both the timing and the manner in which you perform the movement.

4. *Sincerity.* You must feel the purpose of your composition with sufficient intensity to convey this to others.

5. *Confidence.* A skilled performer is poised and in complete control of the situation throughout the time he or she is on stage.

6. *Humility.* No performer should take too seriously the praise he or she receives; there are always faults to be corrected.

7. *Empathy.* Empathy enables the performer to establish a bond of understanding with the audience.

8. *Elegance.* Refinement, grace, and propriety take the performer beyond the mediocre and are appropriate with any theme.

9. *Consistency.* The skilled performer is able to give an excellent performance consistently, even under adverse conditions.

10. *Projection.* Projection in performing means the ability of the performer to hold the attention of the audience throughout the performance, and holding attention is much more difficult than attracting attention.

11. *Magnetism.* Whereas the power to inspire and electrify an audience may be a gift possessed only by a chosen few, the qualities involved are certainly ones that all can develop, to some extent at least, and use to make our performances more stimulating than they would otherwise be. Magnetism is a combination of all the trademarks of a skilled performer. Some of these traits may be acquired through study, observation, instruction, and experience in performing. Others may be intuitive or inherent. Certainly we know that such a performer has a thorough mastery of craftsmanship and technique in his or her field.

Aquatic Art

Is synchronized swimming a sport or an art? It can, and should be *both*. It can also be recreation, entertainment, or exercise, depending upon how you develop the activity. A movement in the water, like a movement on land, can be used for more than one purpose, and in more than one way.

The aquatic artist can be found at all skill levels and in competitive teams, recreational clubs, and performing groups. What is it that identifies the aquatic artist from other competitors or performers?

The aquatic artist may utilize the full spectrum of aquatic skills from which to create compositions: stroking, figures, sculling, floating, and suspension. In addition, various art forms (music, dance, drama, literature, poetry, art) as well as activities such as gymnastics and figure skating may be drawn upon for inspiration and ideas, and elements of these forms may be integrated with aquatic skills.

The aquatic artist understands that there is unlimited opportunity for self-expression and creativeness. He or she explores the possibilities of beautiful, expressive, and graceful movement, perfects the technique, and develops new forms of expression through the aquatic medium.

Aquatic artists view their performance as a gift to anyone watching, and they therefore take care in developing a composition that will be sufficiently meaningful, inspiring, entertaining, or educational to involve the audience. Performing is never done for the sole purpose of displaying skill level.

The aquatic artist choreographs movements that combine to express meaning, rather than simply linking an unrelated series of figures together with transition movements. The music serves to enhance the movement but does not dictate it.

Are you an aquatic artist? Would you like to find out more about using your skills for artistic expression? Membership in the International Academy of Aquatic Art can provide you with information and events that can help you develop your artistic potential.

Formed in 1955, the International Academy of Aquatic Art was established to aid in the development of the creative and artistic aspects of aquatics as a non-competitive, coed activity for all ages. Symposiums and the annual International Festival sponsored by the IAAA stress the importance of basic techniques and how they relate to creative expression. The basic techniques include stroking, sculling, figures, proper breathing, muscular control, and balance. Only after mastering the fundamentals are swimmers ready for advanced techniques that enable them to fully express their ideas in the aquatic medium with finesse. The purpose of the symposiums and Festival is mainly instructional—to help the participants improve in basic skills, to learn new skills, and to apply this knowledge to further their creative and artistic abilities.

The participants in symposiums and Festivals also have the opportunity to present their compositions for evaluation, rating, and award. Compositions are not rated against one another, but they are critiqued against a standard of excellence. Each composition is given a rating based on standards of execution and creativity. If all compositions were of the highest artistic standard, all could receive the highest rating. Similarly, all could receive the lowest rating. A composition is awarded the highest rating (IAAA) if it makes a significant contribution, in the judgment of the critics, to the development of aquatic art.

The IAAA bases all of its activities around three objectives that are stated in its Articles of Incorporation:

1. To recognize and explore the potential of the aquatic medium for truly artistic self-expression and interpretation.
2. To establish an academic environment conducive to the full development of aquatic art forms.
3. To interest the people of the world in participating in the development of aquatic art.

The Academy is concerned with the development of an art form in the aquatic medium, so it must set high artistic standards and demand high levels of achievement from its participants in the process of determining ratings for compositions. Yet this does not mean the Academy is interested only in highly talented swimmers. On the contrary, the Academy welcomes all swimmers (regardless of their artistic talents) to participate in and enjoy aquatic art and to derive the rewards of a creative activity.

For more information about the IAAA, write to Frances Sweeney, IAAA President, 2360 Hedge Row, Northfield, IL 60093.

References

Gundling, B. (1964). *The aquatic art book of water shows*. Cedar Rapids, IA: Author.

Gundling, B. (1966). *Exploring aquatic art*. Cedar Rapids, IA: Author.

Gundling, B. (1971). *Fun with aquatic figure variations*. Cedar Rapids, IA: Author.

Hayes, B.C. (1977). Shallow water lifts. *Aquatic Artist*, **22**, 3-5.

Bibliography

Forbes, M. (1984). *Coaching synchronized swimming effectively.* Champaign, IL: Human Kinetics.

Glinka, D. (1984). Imagine this—Visualization and use of video for practice. *Aquatic Artist,* **30**(1), 4.

Gundling, B. (1972). *Aquatic enchainements and petite compositions.* Cedar Rapids, IA: Author.

Gundling, B. (1976). *Dancing in the water.* Cedar Rapids, IA: Author.

Gundling, B. (1983). Walkover figure variations. *Aquatic Artist,* **29**(1), 5.

Hatten, C. (1984). Figures and choreography: Where's the surprise? *Aquatic Artist,* **30**(3), 5-6.

Haueter, P. (1983). An exercise in developing creative movement. *Aquatic Artist,* **29**(1), 6.

Kahle, V. (1982). Floating skills and patterns. *Aquatic Artist,* **28**(4), 8.

Krack, P. (1986). Elements of creating an aquatic art composition. *Aquatic Artist,* **32**(1), 5.

Lundholm, J.K., & Ruggieri, M.J. (1976). *Introduction to synchronized swimming.* Minneapolis: Burgess.

Schroeder, K. (1981). Doubles and contact figures. *Aquatic Artist,* **27**(4), 7-8.

Sweeney, F. (1975). Choreographing precision stroking compositions. *Aquatic Artist,* **25**(3), 7-8.

VanBuskirk, K.E. (Ed.). (1987). *Coaching intermediate synchronized swimming effectively.* Champaign, IL: Human Kinetics.

VanBuskirk, K., & Scandaliato, K. (Eds.). (1985). *Official 1985-86 synchronized swimming handbook.* Indianapolis: United States Synchronized Swimming.

White, J. (1986). Using synchronized swimming skills for creative expression. *Aquatic Artist,* **32**(4), 5-7.

Index

About the Authors

Beulah Gundling

Beulah Gundling has been a synchronized swimmer for more than 40 years and has performed around the world. She was the first-ever solo champion in 1949 and won the Pan-Am Games' first gold medal for synchronized swimming. Beulah's achievements include earning solo synchro championships nationally and internationally for seven consecutive years, exhibiting in the Olympic Games, and receiving the highest award (the IAAA trophy) in 32 annual International Aquatic Art Festivals. In recognition of her many accomplishments, she was selected as one of the initial honorees of the International Swimming Hall of Fame in Ft. Lauderdale, Florida.

Since retiring undefeated from competitive synchro, Buelah has worked with her husband, Henry, to actively promote swimming as a performing art. *Creative Synchronized Swimming* is her eighth book on the subject. Her other interests include dance, music, walking, reading, and nature.

Jill White with daughter Shannon

Jill White has been active in synchronized swimming and aquatic art since high school, where her love of aquatics began. She was a member of the University of Illinois Aquianas, who became team members of the Aquatic Art Hall of Honor in the International Swimming Hall of Fame. Having chosen aquatics as both her avocation and her profession, she owns and operates Splashworks™ Swim School and sells aquatics supplies. She is on the board of directors of both the IAAA and the Council for National Cooperation in Aquatics and has been a presenter at conferences for both. Jill emphasizes cooperation among agencies and groups in all aquatic sports and programs as the key to their success.

Jill, her swimming coach husband, and their three children live in Sarasota, Florida, where they enjoy many aquatic activities together.